Introduction

Most see the world in binaries: light or dark, life or death, beginning or end. But in the presence of the Mahadev, these boundaries dissolve. To the desperate, he is the Savior—the one who catches the falling Ganges in his hair and drinks the venom of the oceans to preserve the fragile balance of existence. To the fearful, he is the Destroyer—the one who strips away the illusions of the ego and reduces empires to a handful of cold ash.

Yet, as the cosmic clock winds down, we are forced to confront a truth more ancient than time itself:

Is the fire that consumes a forest a tragedy, or is it the only way to make room for new life?

In this journey, we peel back the layers of myth and mystery to uncover the man, the monk, and the monster. We find that the hand raised in blessing is the same hand that wields the trident of annihilation. Shiva: The Savior or The Destroyer is not a search for an answer, but a descent into the beautiful, terrifying reality that he is both and that without his destruction, salvation would have no meaning.

Preface

The concept of Shiva has always occupied a space of profound mystery in the human consciousness. To some, He is the auspicious one, the calm yogi lost in eternal meditation atop Mount Kailash. To others, He is Rudra, the fierce storm-god whose dance can shatter the foundations of the universe.

When I first began writing this book, I found myself circling a single, haunting question: Is Shiva the Saviour or the Destroyer?

As I delved deeper into the myths and the philosophy, I realized that these are not two separate roles, but two sides of the same divine coin. To save a forest, the dry brush must sometimes burn. To birth a new era, the old must perish. Through these pages, I invite you to walk with me through the shadows of destruction and the light of salvation. This book is not just an exploration of a deity, but a reflection on the cycles of our own lives—our endings, our beginnings, and the transformative power that lies within the "in-between."

ABOUT THE ARTIST OF THESE SKETCHES

Banisetti Gayatri is a gifted and deeply intuitive artist whose sketches transcend mere visual representation and enter the realm of spiritual experience. With a masterful command over monochrome tones, shading, and form, she breathes life into divine imagery, particularly the eternal and multifaceted presence of Lord Shiva. Her artwork reflects a rare balance of serenity and power: the meditative calm of Shiva's inner stillness and the cosmic dynamism of Nataraja's dance. Each stroke reveals not only technical precision but also profound devotion, philosophical depth, and emotional sensitivity. The subtle play of light and shadow in her sketches evokes timelessness, inviting the viewer into contemplation rather than observation.

Through charcoal and pencil, Banisetti Gayatri captures the essence of divinity, symbolism, and movement with remarkable clarity and grace. Her work stands as a testament to the belief that art is not merely created, it is realized. This book proudly presents her sketches as visual meditations, offering readers an opportunity to connect with spirituality through art. You can reach to Miss Banisetti Gayatri throughInstagram and can contact her there. Her Instagram ID is @gayatri_arts.

Contents Page No.

Contents Page No.

Contents Page No.

Chapter 1: The Cosmic Paradox

In the vast and intricate tapestry of Hindu mythology, few deities embody a more compelling paradox than Shiva. He is at once the ascetic and the householder, the ultimate creator and the absolute destroyer. This dual nature is not a contradiction but a reflection of the cyclical nature of the cosmos, where creation and destruction are two sides of the same coin. He is revered as the first yogi, the source of all knowledge and meditation, yet he is also the formidable force of dissolution, bringing an end to worlds and illusions. To understand Shiva is to embrace this paradox—to see the profound wisdom in his silence and the cosmic necessity in his fury. He is the ultimate being who exists beyond all classifications, a timeless and formless presence that pervades every particle of existence. His role as the destroyer is not one of malice, but of purification and renewal, clearing the way for new beginnings.

His dualities are physically represented in his very appearance. He is often depicted smeared with **ashes from the cremation grounds**, a symbol of his association with death and dissolution. Yet, these very ashes are seen as a sign of his purity and detachment from the material world. This practice signifies that he is beyond the concepts of life and death, residing in the liminal space where the material body ends and the spiritual journey begins. He sits in deep meditation on **Mount Kailash**, a detached and solitary figure, but is also a loving and devoted husband to Goddess Parvati and a father to their children, Ganesha and Kartikeya. This highlights the balance between spiritual solitude and the responsibilities of worldly life, a profound lesson for anyone seeking harmony.

Another striking paradox is his control over both the most ferocious and the most serene forces. He holds the **Ganga river** in his matted locks, a life-giving force of purity and sustenance, while also wearing a **serpent**, a symbol of destruction and death, around his neck. His **third eye**, located on his forehead, is a source of immense power that can incinerate anything with a fiery gaze, yet it also represents the eye of wisdom and inner vision. This third eye, which remains closed until absolute necessity, is the embodiment of his righteous anger and his capacity for total transformation. Its occasional opening, as we will explore in later chapters, is not a fit of rage, but a deliberate act of divine justice to restore cosmic order.

These seemingly contradictory attributes are what make Shiva such a complex and revered figure. He is not merely a god to be worshipped, but a philosophical concept to be contemplated—a reminder that life and death, creation and destruction, stillness and action are all interconnected and essential parts of a single, cosmic rhythm. He is the divine embodiment of what is known as **Lila**, the cosmic play of existence. Every form he takes, every story told about him, and every symbol he carries, serves to illustrate that the universe is in a perpetual state of flux, and that change, even destructive change, is fundamental to its continued existence. His destructive aspect is never an act of malice, but a divine intervention to clear the way for new beginnings, ensuring the endless cycle of existence continues.

Perhaps the most potent symbol of Shiva's paradox is his form as **Nataraja**, the cosmic dancer. This iconic representation captures the entire process of the universe's creation, preservation, and dissolution in a single, dynamic posture. With one leg raised in a powerful dance step, he balances on a dwarf demon named **Apasmara**, who represents ignorance and illusion. The dance itself is a metaphor for the universe in motion, with every beat of his drum creating life and every flicker of the flame in his hand signaling dissolution. The ring of fire surrounding him is the cosmic fire of destruction, but it is also the source of new life. In this one form, Shiva embodies the entire cosmic cycle. The **damaru** (drum) in his upper right hand represents the sound of creation, the very vibration from which the universe emerged. The flame in his upper left hand signifies destruction, the force that dissolves all forms into nothingness. His lower right hand is in the abhaya mudra, a gesture of fearlessness, assuring his devotees that they are protected. The lower left-hand points to his raised foot, inviting devotees to seek refuge in him, a symbol of liberation. The dance of **Nataraja** is a profound summary of Shiva's role: he is the eternal source of energy, continuously bringing the cosmos into being, sustaining it, and then dissolving it, only to begin the cycle anew.

Further, the duality of Shiva is perfectly captured in his form as **Ardhanarishvara**, a composite of himself and his consort, Parvati. This half-male, half-female form is a deep philosophical statement on the ultimate unity of opposites. The masculine principle, **Purusha**, represents pure consciousness and stillness, while the feminine principle, **Prakriti**, represents active energy and matter. The union of these two principles is what gives rise to all of creation. In **Ardhanarishvara**, the left half is Parvati, adorned with a graceful form, a sari, and feminine ornaments, while the right half is Shiva, with matted hair, a tiger skin, and his trident. This form transcends gender and polarity, illustrating that the universe is born from the harmonious interplay of masculine and feminine energies. It is a powerful reminder that every individual, regardless of gender, contains both these energies, and that true completeness comes from their integration. It is a symbol of cosmic balance, of the sacred marriage between stillness and motion, and of the idea that a whole is created from the union of two seemingly separate parts. The legend behind this form speaks to Parvati's desire to become one with Shiva, to understand the totality of his being, and his granting of her wish. It is a story of love, devotion, and the spiritual aspiration to merge with the ultimate reality.

In essence, Shiva is not a simple deity with a singular function. He is the embodiment of the universe itself, a mirror reflecting the grand, paradoxical nature of existence. He teaches that life and death are not enemies but partners in an eternal dance, that stillness and action are two sides of the same coin, and that true power lies in the ability to accept and contain all aspects of reality, both beautiful and terrifying. His every symbol, from the crescent moon to the sacred serpent, from his meditative pose to his cosmic dance, invites us to contemplate the profound truths that lie beyond simple observation. He is the paradox, and in understanding him, we begin to understand the deeper rhythms of our own lives and the universe we inhabit.

To truly understand whether Lord Mahadev is a saviour or a destroyer, we must first journey through the story of his life and the depth of his eternal existence.

Chapter 2: The Pillar of Infinity: A Test of Truth

In the beginning, before the myriad of stars and galaxies had found their place, there was a void. From this void emerged two great lords: Lord Vishnu, the preserver, and Lord Brahma, the creator. They were the most powerful beings in all of existence, and yet, in their solitude, an ancient debate began. Their pride, a force as potent as the cosmos itself, kindled a conflict over their supremacy.

"I am the ultimate source," declared Brahma, who sat upon his lotus throne, speaking with the authority of the universe's very architect. "From me, all of creation flows. All things you see, from the mountains to the mortals, are a result of my creative will. You are but a secondary force, maintaining what I have made."

"You are the creator, yes," replied Vishnu, resting upon the cosmic serpent Shesha, his form serene and timeless. "But you can only create what I preserve. Without me, your creations would crumble into dust. I am the very force that holds the cosmos together, and thus, I am the supreme being. Your creation would be a fleeting illusion without my sustaining power."

As their argument grew, the very balance of the universe seemed to tremble. Their words, charged with divine power, echoed through the vast emptiness. It was at this moment, to their astonishment, that a third presence manifested. Between them, from the ground of the void, a colossal pillar of pure, radiant light erupted. It was a fiery column, a **lingam**, that stretched endlessly towards the heavens and plunged into the depths of the abyss below. Its brilliance was so intense it outshone the suns of a thousand universes, and its form was so magnificent it humbled the two proud gods.

Realizing they were in the presence of a greater power, Vishnu and Brahma temporarily set aside their feud. In a silent agreement, they decided to find the end of this pillar of light. The one who could reach its end would prove to be the most powerful of the three. It was a test of supremacy that neither could refuse.

Brahma, with his four faces, transformed into a great white swan, an embodiment of purity and flight. With a powerful beat of his wings, he soared into the sky, his eyes fixed on the pillar's top. He flew for thousands upon thousands of years, passing through countless celestial realms and galaxies, but the column of light continued to extend endlessly above him, showing no sign of its peak. Frustrated and with his pride wounded, he decided to turn back. On his descent, he encountered a **Ketaki flower** falling from the pillar. He asked the flower where it was from and the flower said it was from the top of the Lingam. Brahma then concocted a plan to get the flower to lie for him.

Meanwhile, Vishnu took the form of a wild boar, its tusks as sharp as thunderbolts and its strength as great as a hundred mountains. He burrowed downwards, tearing through the cosmic soil and plunging into the blackness of the netherworld. He, too, descended for a countless age, yet the lingam's base remained a distant and unreachable goal. Unlike Brahma, Vishnu returned, exhausted and humbled by his fruitless journey, and he admitted his failure.

When they met, Brahma, consumed by his pride, lied and claimed to have found the top of the column, using the Ketaki flower as his false witness. At that very moment, the fiery column of light began to recede, and from within its core emerged the great Lord Shiva. His body was smeared with ash, his hair was matted, and he wore a serpent around his neck. He was both ancient and eternal, peaceful and fearsome.

Shiva's voice, like the very sound of creation, thundered through the void. He **cursed Brahma** for his deceit and banished the Ketaki flower from being used in his worship as a punishment for its complicity in the lie. But he honoured Vishnu for his truthfulness and declared that Vishnu would be revered by all for his honesty. Shiva revealed that he was the **Lingam** itself, the unmanifested form of the absolute, and that all of creation was merely a manifestation of his boundless energy. From that day forth, the Lingam became the primary symbol of his worship, a reminder to all beings that the Lord of all is without beginning and without end.

Chapter 3: The Saga of Mahadeva and Sati

In the pantheon of gods, there existed a divine rivalry as old as the mountains and as deep as the seas. It was the chasm between the pragmatic, rule-bound King Daksha, a son of Brahma, and the wild, untamed ascetic, Lord Shiva. Daksha, the proud and esteemed Prajapati, took pride in his lineage and his strict adherence to cosmic law. Shiva, however, resided on Mount Kailash—smeared in ash, adorned with serpents, and immersed in deep meditation—an enigmatic figure who seemed to defy and mock Daksha's conventions. To Daksha, Shiva was a rogue, a dishevelled recluse unworthy of respect.

Yet, fate, with its subtle and inescapable hand, had a different plan. King Daksha had a daughter, Sati, the embodiment of grace and purity. From her earliest days, Sati's heart was not drawn to the finery of her father's court or the promise of a glorious marriage to a powerful king. Instead, her soul yearned for the distant Lord of Kailash. Tales of his compassion, his dance of creation and destruction, and his profound wisdom captivated her. She performed rigorous austerities, her devotion a beacon of pure love, hoping to win the heart of the great Mahadeva.

Moved by her unwavering love, Shiva descended from his abode. He appeared before her, a vision of paradox—frightening yet beautiful, destructive yet serene. Her penance bore fruit, and the love between them blossomed, a bond that transcended all mortal and immortal understanding. When Shiva sought her hand in marriage,

Daksha's pride shattered. He fumed at the very idea, seeing it as an ultimate insult. But Sati's resolve was as unshakable as a mountain, and with the support of Brahma, their marriage was solemnized. In an act of open defiance and contempt, Daksha refused to attend the wedding, forever severing ties with his beloved daughter and her enigmatic husband.

Time passed, and the rift between Daksha and Shiva only deepened. Daksha's scorn grew into a festering hatred. He decided to perform a grand yagna, a sacred fire sacrifice of immense importance, to which he invited every god, goddess, celestial being, and sage in the universe—every one, that is, except Shiva. He sought not just to perform a ritual but to publicly humiliate his son-in-law, to prove his superiority and diminish Shiva's divine stature in the eyes of the cosmos.

Sati, upon hearing of the magnificent yagna, was torn. Her family was there, and a part of her longed to be with them, to bridge the distance her father had created. Despite Shiva's gentle counsel that attending an uninvited gathering could only lead to dishonour and pain, Sati, out of love for her family and a sense of duty, insisted on going. With a heavy heart, Shiva permitted her to go, guarded by his Ganas.

Sati arrived at the yagna, a lone figure in a sea of celebration. She was met not with warmth but with silent scorn and pointed whispers. She sought out her father, hoping for a kind word, a gesture of reconciliation. Instead, Daksha's gaze was cold, and his words were venomous. He publicly and brutally insulted Shiva, mocking his appearance, his followers, and his very nature. The insults were not just aimed at Shiva, but at the very essence of Sati's love and her choice. She felt a burning, unbearable anguish, a profound grief for the father who rejected her love and the husband whose honour was being desecrated.

The flames of the yagna roared, but within Sati, a fiercer fire ignited. Her face drained of color as she declared that she could not bear to live in a body born of such a father, a father who had blasphemed her divine husband. With a terrible vow, she closed her eyes, focused her immense yogic power, and summoned the internal fire of her soul. The yagna hall fell into a stunned silence as Sati, engulfed in her own divine conflagration, immolated her physical form. Her sacrifice was not an act of weakness but of ultimate power, a testament to her devotion and a final, shattering protest.

The news of Sati's immolation reached Shiva in a flash of divine horror. His grief transcended all cosmic boundaries. It was a primal, all-consuming pain that transformed into a fury so absolute it threatened to unravel the very fabric of existence. From a single lock of his hair, Shiva created Virabhadra and Bhadrakali, two ferocious beings born of pure wrath. He commanded them to destroy Daksha's yagna and everything in their path. The pair descended upon the hall, a force of nature, laying waste to the sacrifice, scattering the gods, and beheading the arrogant Daksha. As the gods watched the chaos and the death of their king, they trembled with fear. They realized the folly of their silence and begged for Shiva's mercy. They pleaded with him to restore Daksha's life, to bring balance back to the universe. Shiva, seeing their remorse and his own righteous anger now satiated, felt his immense power shift from destruction to restoration. He approached the lifeless body of his father-in-law. Finding a goat's head among the sacrificed animals, he joined it to Daksha's body, restoring his life. Humbled and forever marked by the lesson of Shiva's power, Daksha, with his new head, prostrated himself before Shiva, finally acknowledging his greatness.

But this was not enough for Shiva's grief. He still carried Sati's lifeless body and began his furious Tandava, the cosmic dance of destruction. His grief-stricken steps shook the cosmos, threatening to bring about the end of the world. The gods, terrified, appealed to Lord Vishnu to intervene. With his divine discus, Vishnu severed Sati's body into fifty-one pieces. As each piece fell to the earth, Shiva's frenzied dance began to slow, his rage giving way to sorrow. The spots where Sati's body parts landed became the revered holy sites known as the Shakti Peethas, eternal shrines of the Divine Mother.

Shiva, his mind finally at peace but his heart shattered, returned to his deep meditation on Mount Kailash, guarding his grief. He knew Sati would one day return to him, reborn as Parvati, daughter of the mountains, to complete their eternal cycle of love. But for now, the universe waited, silent and humbled, in the wake of a love that had defied a king and ended a creation, only to begin anew.

Chapter 4: The Third Eye Awakens

The cosmos was left in a state of profound silence following the cataclysmic events of Daksha's yagna. The divine realm, once bustling with ritual and power, now moved with a new sense of solemnity. On Mount Kailash, the great Mahadeva, Shiva, was a figure of absolute sorrow. He had returned to his meditation, not in bliss, but in a profound and aching grief. His eyes were closed, lost in the memory of his beloved Sati, and the world held its breath in his silence. It was a silence that spoke of loss so deep, no force in the universe could disturb him. The gods, humbled by his fury and sorrow, knew that to approach him now was to risk the wrath of a still-wounded soul.

But even as sorrow consumed the Lord of Kailash, a new hope was taking form in the world of mortals. From the union of King Himavat, the Lord of the Himalayas, and his queen, Mena, a daughter was born. Her beauty was said to rival the snow-capped peaks and her spirit was as pure as the mountain air. She was named Parvati, "She of the Mountain." As she grew, Parvati heard the same tales of Lord Shiva that had so captivated Sati in her previous life. Her heart, a vessel of memory, instinctively recognized him. She loved him with an innate, unshakable devotion, a love that was not new, but eternal. Her single desire was to serve him and to be by his side.

The divine beings, meanwhile, were facing a grave crisis. The demon Tarakasura, blessed with a boon that made him virtually invincible—he could only be defeated by the son of Shiva—was wreaking havoc upon the heavens and the earth. With Shiva lost in his desolate meditation, the gods saw no way to produce such a son. They realized the fate of the universe rested on one impossible task: they had to awaken Shiva from his trance and ignite within him the passion for marriage once more.

Knowing the futility of a direct approach, the gods turned to the one being with a chance of success: Kamadev, the God of Love. Kamadev, with his bow of sugarcane and arrows tipped with flowers, was tasked with a mission of unimaginable peril. He was to pierce Shiva's heart with the arrows of love, to make him feel desire again. Kamadev approached with trepidation, accompanied by his wife Rati and his friend Vasanta, the personification of spring. As he drew his bow, a gentle and sweet aura of love and longing filled the air. Flowers bloomed, and a gentle breeze whispered through the trees. Even the gods who had come to witness the event felt a new tenderness in their hearts.

Just as Parvati, in her role as a devoted maiden, was walking towards Shiva to offer him flowers, Kamadev took his shot. He aimed his most potent arrow at Shiva's heart. The arrow struck, but the effect was not what was intended. A flicker of emotion, a spark of fleeting desire, passed over Shiva's face for a fleeting moment. But it was not love that came to him. It was a searing, consuming rage. He had been disturbed from his meditation, and the serenity he had cultivated to guard his grief was shattered. A single, furious eye opened on his forehead—the third eye, a force of immense destruction. A beam of fire erupted from it, searing the air and instantly reducing Kamadev to a pile of ash.

The world was once again plunged into chaos and sorrow. Kamadev's wife, Rati, wept inconsolably. Parvati, standing by, witnessed the terrible power of Shiva's wrath and understood the folly of the gods' plan. She realized that Shiva could not be won through external means, not through beauty, or through the fleeting magic of love. He could only be won through a devotion as profound and a spiritual power as immense as his own. With a new resolve, she set a new path for herself. She would not simply wait for Shiva, but would become worthy of him, a true partner in spirit. She left her palatial home and her family's comforts, determined to perform a penance so severe, it would shake the foundations of the universe and prove her unwavering love for the Lord of the Universe.

Chapter 5: The Penance of Parvati and her Final Test and Reunion with Mahadev

After witnessing the searing power of Shiva's third eye and the tragic fate of Kama, Parvati understood that her path to her beloved lay not through gentle gestures or physical attraction, but through a spiritual devotion so pure and so absolute that it would earn his respect. With unwavering resolve, she left her father's palace, leaving behind all royal comforts and material possessions. She sought a solitary life of extreme austerity in the forest, determined to win Shiva's heart by becoming his equal in spiritual power.

Her tapasya (penance) was a sight of unparalleled dedication. She began by living a life of simplicity, subsisting only on fruits and vegetables that grew wild. As her resolve deepened, she gave up food entirely, eating only leaves that fell from the trees. For her unwavering asceticism, she earned the name **Aparna**, meaning "one without leaves." Her penance grew even more severe. For years, she stood in the blistering heat of the sun, her body scorched and weathered. She endured the **Panchagni tapas**, the penance of the five fires, where she sat surrounded by four blazing bonfires with the fierce sun as the fifth fire above her head. For months on end, she stood on a single foot, her body emaciated and frail, yet her mind remained a fortress of concentration, fixed solely on Mahadeva. The gods, watching from the heavens, were in awe of her devotion, knowing no one, mortal or immortal, had ever performed such a powerful penance.

After many long years, Shiva, who was privy to all events in the cosmos, knew that Parvati's penance had reached its climax. Moved by her unwavering devotion, he decided to test her one last time. He approached her disguised as an old, wizened Brahmin. His face was wrinkled, his body frail, and he carried a walking stick. As he drew near, he spoke to Parvati in a seemingly kind but critical tone.

"Child, why do you perform such harsh austerities for that strange ascetic of Kailash, Shiva? He is a wild recluse, smeared in ash, living among ghosts and serpents. He has no home, no worldly possessions, and he is unpredictable in his moods. A beautiful and worthy maiden like you should marry a powerful god or a noble king, not a wanderer."

Parvati's face, which had been serene in her meditation, grew angry. She looked at the old Brahmin with a fierce gaze. "You speak with the ignorance of a man who does not understand true divinity!" she declared. "You only see the outward appearance, not the pure heart of the one you insult. Shiva is the ultimate being, the very embodiment of the cosmos. He is not a vagabond; he is beyond all worldly things. I love him for who he is, and if you cannot speak of him with reverence, then I have no desire to speak with you. Leave this place at once!"

With her final words, Parvati turned to leave, her resolve firm to not listen to another word of blasphemy against her lord. As she turned, the old Brahmin's form began to shimmer. He transformed, his frail body replaced by the majestic form of Lord Shiva himself, serene and radiant.

Parvati froze, unable to speak, her heart filled with shock and joy.

Shiva smiled gently. "My dear Parvati," he said. "I apologize for my words. I only wanted to test your devotion, and your love has passed every trial. You have truly won me, not by beauty or charm, but by the spiritual power of your love and faith. You are my Shakti, the one I have been waiting for."

The heavens rejoiced at their reunion. The marriage was celebrated with a grandeur that shook the cosmos, uniting not just two beings, but the fundamental forces of the universe—the masculine and the feminine, the static and the dynamic, the stillness and the energy. Parvati, the eternal soul of Sati, had finally re-joined her Mahadeva, bringing balance and harmony back to all of creation.

Chapter 6: The Birth of a Warrior

After ages of profound penance and unwavering devotion, Goddess Parvati finally won the heart of Lord Shiva. Their divine union was a cosmic event of immense power, a purposeful convergence of the male and female energies of the universe. From this union was born a being of unparalleled might and brilliance, a celestial warrior destined to be the commander-in-chief of the gods' army: **Kartikeya**, also known as Skanda, Murugan, and Subramanya.

His birth was not a simple event. It was the direct fulfilment of a celestial prophecy that only a son of Shiva could have the strength to defeat the demon king **Tarakasura**. The demon, through immense penance, had earned a boon of invincibility from Lord Brahma, and had used it to conquer the three worlds and drive the gods from their heavens. With the birth of Kartikeya, the gods saw their only hope, and they knew it was all according to Shiva's divine plan.

From the moment he was born, Kartikeya was destined for greatness. The gods and celestial beings themselves became his teachers, nurturing his immense power and training him in the art of war. He was taught and guided by the Saptarishi, the seven great sages. But it was his father, Lord Shiva, who took on the most significant role. In the sacred stillness of Mount Kailash, Mahadeva himself imparted the divine knowledge of combat to his son. Shiva taught him not just how to wield weapons, but the very **philosophy of war**, the does and don'ts of battle, the difference between righteousness and vengeance, and the importance of using power for protection.

The prophesied final battle began as Kartikeya, a beacon of divine power, led the celestial army against Tarakasura and his demonic hordes. The clash was epic, shaking the very foundations of the three worlds. Tarakasura was immense in his might, and his army was a sea of malice, but against them stood the gods, led by their new general. Shiva himself, from his place on Mount Kailash, watched with an all-seeing eye, his presence a source of immense power for his son.

The fight between Kartikeya and Tarakasura was a spectacle of divine fury. The demon, for all his boons, was no match for the divine energy that flowed through Kartikeya. The celestial warrior, with his twelve arms, fought with the ferocity of a thousand thunderstorms. He moved with a speed that was a blur to the eyes of mortals, his sacred spear, the **Vel**, a flash of pure light.

With a powerful, final strike of the Vel, Kartikeya pierced Tarakasura's heart, ending his reign of terror. As the demon's body fell, its immense form crumbled into dust, and light and balance were restored to the universe. Shiva's role in the death of Tarakasura was a subtle but profound act of creation, providing the universe with the very warrior it needed to defeat the unstoppable force of destruction.

Chapter 7: The Blue-Throated Saviour

The title of "Destroyer" often conjures images of unbridled rage and ruin, but in the context of Shiva, destruction is a sacred and necessary act of cosmic purification. To understand this, we must look to the ancient myth of the **Samudra Manthan**, the Churning of the Cosmic Ocean. This epic tale is not merely a story of gods and demons but a profound allegory for the cosmic process of creation, sustenance, and the necessary confrontation with negativity.

The story begins with the gods losing their power and vitality due to a curse from the sage Durvasa. To regain their strength and achieve immortality, they sought the help of Vishnu, the preserver. Vishnu advised them to churn the great cosmic ocean of milk. However, the task was too immense for the gods alone, so they formed a temporary and uneasy alliance with the demons. Together, they used **Mount Mandara** as their churning rod and the great serpent **Vasuki** as the churning rope. Mount Mandara was placed on the back of the cosmic turtle **Kurma** (an avatar of Vishnu) to keep it from sinking.

The churning began, a monumental effort that lasted for a thousand years. As the ocean was churned, it first released a torrent of divine treasures. Out came the celestial cow **Kamadhenu**, the goddess of wealth **Lakshmi**, the wish-fulfilling tree **Parijata**, the enchanting celestial nymphs, and other precious items. The gods and demons eagerly divided these treasures, their temporary truce holding strong. However, the churning soon brought forth a darker and more terrifying substance: a deadly poison called **Halahala**.

This poison was so potent that its fumes began to spread throughout the three worlds, threatening to consume all life—gods, demons, and mortals alike. The atmosphere turned suffocating, the seas began to boil, and the stars dimmed. Panic ensued. The gods and demons, who had so eagerly clamored for the treasures, now fled in terror from the Halahala, a byproduct of their quest for immortality. In their desperation, they realized their folly and sought refuge in Shiva, the only one with the power and detachment to handle such a malevolent force. They found him on Mount Kailash, serene and detached, untouched by the chaos below.

Seeing the plight of all beings, Shiva, without a moment's hesitation, moved to save the universe. He did not seek to destroy the poison or cast it away, as either act would have caused more destruction. Instead, he gathered the entire quantity of Halahala into his hands, forming it into a single, deadly ball. As he prepared to drink it, his consort, Parvati, fearing for his life, gripped his throat to prevent the poison from descending into his body and reaching his stomach, which would have meant the end of the universe. The poison remained lodged in his throat, a permanent testament to his sacrifice, turning it a deep shade of blue. Thus, Shiva earned the name **Neelakantha**, the "blue-throated one." This act was a profound sacrifice, demonstrating that a true saviour is one who is willing to absorb the suffering and toxicity of others, rather than merely fighting it from a distance.

The symbolism of this story extends far beyond a single event. It is a testament to the idea that true salvation sometimes requires the willingness to face and absorb the very things that threaten to destroy us. The poison represents the collective evils and impurities of the world—ignorance, ego, greed, and attachment—and Shiva's act of holding it in his throat symbolizes his role as the ultimate cleanser. He does not simply destroy these negative forces; he takes them into himself, preventing them from corrupting the rest of the universe. This story highlights the immense compassion and benevolence that lie beneath his often-austere and destructive exterior.

This concept is reflected in other aspects of his appearance as well. The **serpent Vasuki**, which had been used to churn the ocean and spew forth the poison, is seen coiled around Shiva's neck as a permanent adornment. This isn't just a physical ornament; it represents his mastery over destructive and venomous forces, a symbol that he has tamed the very chaos that threatened the cosmos. Similarly, the **crescent moon** on his head symbolizes his control over time and his serene, detached nature, reminding us that even amidst chaos, a higher order prevails. His **matted hair**, from which the sacred river Ganga flows, further underscores his role as a preserver and giver of life, showcasing the paradox that even as he contains the destructive poison, he also holds the life-giving waters. The story of Ganga's descent is a legend in itself, where she fell from the heavens and Shiva's locks broke her fall, saving the earth from her immense force. This duality reinforces the idea that Shiva's destructive power is not an end in itself, but a part of a larger, harmonious cosmic cycle. His stillness and meditative state amidst the chaos of the Halahala demonstrate that true power comes not from aggression, but from an unwavering inner calm and self-control.

Ultimately, the story of Halahala is a cornerstone of his identity as a saviour. His blue throat is a constant reminder that he is the great benefactor who takes on the suffering and toxicity of the universe, offering a path to renewal and new creation. His act was not about ending something, but about saving everything, proving that the destroyer can also be the ultimate redeemer. This myth teaches us that even in the pursuit of great things, we must be prepared for unexpected dangers, and that the greatest strength is not in avoiding chaos, but in having the courage and compassion to face it and contain it for the good of all.

Chapter 8: The Lord of New Beginnings

In the serene, meditative quietude of Mount Kailash, Goddess Parvati felt a deep sense of separation from her husband, Lord Shiva, who was often lost in his profound, timeless meditation. Out of a yearning for a companion, she decided to create a son. Taking the **ubtan**, a sacred paste of turmeric, sandalwood, and other fragrant herbs used for her bath, she molded a perfect, divine form of a boy. As she breathed her life force into the figure, he came to life, a manifestation of her own divine will and a testament to her creative power. This was the birth of **Binayaka**.

Filled with the immense love of a mother, Parvati gave her son a simple, yet sacred, task. "My dear , stand guard at the entrance to my chambers. I am going to bath, and no one, not even the gods, shall pass you, Binayaka", with a heart overflowing with loyalty, took his position and became a formidable, unwavering guardian. He was bound only by his mother's command, a symbol of the profound duty of a son.

A short time later, Lord Shiva, returning from his long meditation, approached his home. He was greeted by a boy he had never seen before, who stood firmly in his way. "I am sorry, sir," Binayaka said with a voice of gentle but unyielding authority. "My mother is inside, and she has instructed me to let no one pass."

Shiva, the supreme being, was taken aback. This was his home, and yet, a strange boy dared to stop him. The conversation quickly escalated. When Shiva's loyal army, the **Ganas**, appeared and tried to remove the boy, Binayaka, imbued with Parvati's cosmic power, single-handedly defeated them all. He was a force to be reckoned with, a divine creation capable of protecting his mother's honor against all odds.

Seeing his army defeated, Shiva's divine fury, the same cosmic force that brings about the end of an age, rose to a terrifying peak. Still unaware that this was his own son, he raised his fearsome trident, the **Trishula**, and in a single, powerful motion, he beheaded Binayaka. The boy's body fell to the ground, lifeless.

When Parvati emerged and saw the tragic scene, her grief and rage shook the cosmos to its very core. Her sorrow was so profound that she threatened to destroy all of creation. The gods and goddesses, terrified by her destructive power, pleaded with Shiva to console her. Here, Shiva's true nature as a **saviour** came to the forefront. He had inadvertently caused this tragedy, but his benevolent role was to restore balance and life. Realizing the grave error he had made, Shiva promised to revive Binayaka. He sent his Ganas to find the head of the first living creature they encountered. They returned with the head of a powerful elephant, which Shiva placed on Binayaka's body, bringing him back to life with a new form. This act was not a simple restoration; it was a cosmic transformation, a rebirth that elevated Binayaka to a new, more profound status.

With Binayaka restored, Shiva embraced him and declared him the leader of his Ganas, giving him the name **Ganapati or Ganesh**, the lord of all beings. He also decreed that before any new venture, Ganesh must be worshipped first, forever cementing his place as the god of new beginnings and the remover of obstacles. The tale is a powerful lesson that even the most seemingly destructive actions of a deity can be part of a larger, benevolent plan to restore harmony and create something new and profound.

Chapter 9: Mahakal, The Conqueror of Time

The great sage **Mrikandu** and his wife, consumed by their deep desire for a child, devoted years of their lives to rigorous penance, their unwavering faith directed at Lord Shiva. Their devotion was so profound that it touched the very heart of the supreme deity. Pleased, Shiva appeared before them and presented a cosmic choice that would define their destiny. "You may have a hundred foolish sons with long lives," Shiva said, his voice echoing with divine grace, "or a single virtuous and wise son with a life of just sixteen years." Without a moment's hesitation, Mrikandu and his wife chose the latter, prioritizing virtue and wisdom over a long but hollow life. The couple was blessed with a son, whom they named **Markandeya**, a child destined to live a life of brilliance and piety, yet with a predetermined, short end.

Markandeya grew up to be everything his parents had wished for. He mastered the Vedas and Shastras at an impossibly young age, his devotion to Lord Shiva shining brightly for all to see. Yet, as his sixteenth birthday drew near, a shadow of despair fell upon his parents. Their joy was now tinged with the pain of his impending fate. When they finally revealed the painful truth to their son, Markandeya's reaction was not one of fear, but of profound resolve. He consoled his parents, reminding them that the soul is eternal and a life of devotion is a life well lived, regardless of its length. He then intensified his worship, seeking refuge in the divine, spending his final days in deep meditation, chanting the powerful **Mahamrityunjaya Mantra**, a hymn dedicated to conquering death itself.

On the day of his sixteenth birthday, **Yama**, the fearsome god of death, arrived on his black buffalo to claim Markandeya's soul. His servants had already tried and failed, unable to approach the young sage due to the radiating power of his devotion. Yama, angered, cast his noose to pull the young soul from his body. But in his final act of unwavering faith, Markandeya clung to the **Shiva Lingam**, crying out for his Lord's protection. The noose, meant only for Markandeya's soul, also encircled the sacred Lingam.

This act was an affront to the cosmic order, and it awoke Shiva's divine wrath. The earth trembled, the heavens darkened, and from the Lingam, Shiva emerged in his most fearsome form, **Mahakal**, the conqueror of time. His eyes burned with a righteous fury. "How dare you," Shiva roared at Yama, "touch my true devotee, who has surrendered completely to me!" In a swift and powerful motion, Shiva struck Yama down with his foot, subduing the god of death and stopping the flow of time itself. The gods, terrified of a world without death, pleaded with Shiva to restore Yama to life. Shiva, ever the benevolent saviour, relented and brought Yama back, but with one condition: Markandeya would remain a **Chiranjivi**, an immortal, forever sixteen.

The tale stands as a testament to the boundless power of devotion and Lord Shiva's promise to protect those who seek refuge in him, transcending even the finality of death. It illustrates that true faith can alter destiny, and even the laws of the universe can be bent for a sincere devotee.

Chapter 10: The 28 Incarnations of Lord Shiva

Lord Shiva, the great Mahadev, is revered in countless forms and manifestations. While he is often associated with destruction, many of his incarnations, or avatars, were taken to protect the innocent, punish the arrogant, and restore balance to the universe. These forms are born from his profound compassion and his unyielding commitment to dharma. Each of the **19 major incarnations** of Shiva reveals a unique facet of his role as a saviour.

1. Piplad

The **Piplad** avatar was born to save humanity from the malefic influence of the planet **Shani** (Saturn). Piplad was born from a fig tree and was raised by Sage Dadhichi. His motive was to punish Shani for causing suffering to his father, Dadhichi, in his infancy. He cursed Shani to become powerless to children under the age of 16. Through this act, Shiva as Piplad saved children from the most dangerous periods of Shani's wrath.

2. Nandi

Nandi is the divine bull and the most beloved of Shiva's devotees. In some traditions, he is considered a direct incarnation of Shiva himself, manifested to serve as his eternal vehicle and gatekeeper. His purpose as a saviour is to serve as a symbol of eternal devotion and strength, guiding followers on the path to righteousness. Nandi's presence in Shiva's temples protects devotees from evil and grants them access to the divine.

3. Virabhadra

Born from Shiva's fury after the death of Sati, **Virabhadra's** motive was righteous revenge. He appeared to punish the arrogance of Daksha, Sati's father, who had insulted Shiva and caused his daughter's demise. Virabhadra's destructive power was not for chaos, but for justice, to re-establish cosmic order and protect the honor of the divine.

4. Bhairava

Bhairava is a fierce manifestation of Shiva whose purpose is to punish those who disrespect the divine. His origin story involves him beheading one of Lord Brahma's heads to curb his ego. Bhairava's motive as a saviour is to protect the cosmos from arrogance and ignorance. He is revered as the guardian of temples and the one who removes sins and fears from his devotees, destroying their inner darkness.

5. Sharabha

Sharabha is a unique incarnation that arose to contain the unbridled rage of Vishnu's Narasimha avatar. After defeating the demon Hiranyakashipu, Narasimha's fury threatened to destroy the universe. Shiva, as Sharabha—a hybrid of a bird, lion, and human—fought and pacified Narasimha. His sole motive was to save the cosmos from annihilation and restore equilibrium.

6. Grihapati

Grihapati was a young boy who was born to a righteous couple as a blessing from Shiva. When he was born, astrologers predicted a short lifespan for him. To save his life, he went to Banaras to perform penance. His steadfast devotion to Shiva saved him from death, and he was blessed with a long life. The motive behind this incarnation is to show that sincere devotion and faith can conquer even the fate determined by the stars.

7. Yatinath

The **Yatinath** form was taken by Shiva to test the hospitality of a tribal couple, Aahuk and Aahuka. He appeared to them as a poor hermit and requested shelter for the night. Despite their meager resources, the couple welcomed him with open hearts. Yatinath's motive was to reward their selflessness and devotion. When he was ready to leave, he blessed the couple with immense wealth and eternal salvation, showing that true devotion is rewarded.

8. Sureshwar

This form was taken by Shiva to save the celestial king Indra from the arrogance of his own ego. **Sureshwar**, a sage-like figure, appeared before Indra. When Indra's pride led him to disrespect the sage, Shiva revealed his true form and humbled the king. The motive was to teach Indra a lesson in humility, saving him from the consequences of his own arrogance.

9. Brahmachari

When Shiva and Parvati were to be married, Shiva appeared as a young sage, or **Brahmachari**, to test Parvati's devotion. He came to her and spoke ill of Shiva, but Parvati's love remained unwavering. The motive was to prove Parvati's pure love to the world and to save her from any self-doubt. By accepting her devotion, he showed that true love and faith are the greatest virtues.

10. Avadhut

Avadhut is a form of Shiva as an enlightened sage, who transcends all worldly attachments. He appeared to a king who had become too arrogant about his knowledge. The motive was to humble the king and teach him about true spiritual wisdom. Shiva, as Avadhut, showed that real knowledge comes not from books or power but from spiritual detachment.

11. Hanuman

In some traditions, **Hanuman** is considered the eleventh incarnation of Shiva, born to serve Lord Rama. His purpose was to assist in the defeat of the demon king Ravana and the restoration of dharma. Hanuman's motive was to serve, and through his selfless devotion and strength, he saved Sita and helped establish a righteous kingdom.

12. Nateshwar

Nateshwar, or Nataraja, is the cosmic dancer. His dance is not just for entertainment; it is the source of all movement in the universe. The motive behind this incarnation is to save creation by continuously recreating and preserving it through his rhythmic dance. The dance of Nataraja symbolizes the liberation of souls from the veil of ignorance.

13. Bhikshuvarya

In this form, Shiva appeared as a divine mendicant who saves beings by liberating them from their worldly attachments. He is often depicted with a begging bowl, symbolizing that he has transcended all material desires. His motive is to show humanity that true wealth lies in spiritual freedom and detachment.

14. Kshemaka

Kshemaka is a form of Shiva who protects his devotees from harm and guides them through difficult times. His name itself means "one who is peaceful." The motive of this incarnation is to provide security and comfort to those who seek his refuge. He is a protector who ensures the well-being and prosperity of his followers.

15. Durvasa

Sage **Durvasa** is known for his short temper, which is often mistaken for a flaw. However, he is an incarnation of Shiva whose anger serves a purpose. His motive is to test the devotion and patience of great beings. By putting them through trials, he purifies their souls and saves them from the spiritual downfall of pride.

16. Khandoba

Khandoba is a popular regional deity in Maharashtra and Karnataka, worshipped as a manifestation of Shiva. His motive as a saviour is to fight against evil forces and protect the righteous. He is a compassionate protector who grants wishes to his devotees and defends them from all forms of danger, both spiritual and physical.

17. Kirateshwar Avatar

Shiva appeared as a tribal hunter to test the valor and skill of the Pandava prince Arjuna. After a duel, Shiva revealed his true form and gifted Arjuna the divine weapon, *Pashupatastra*.

18. Yaksheswar

Shiva took this form to humble the gods who became arrogant after they had helped in the churning of the ocean. He appeared as a giant Yaksha to show them their pride was misplaced.

19. Vrishbha

The **Vrishbha** avatar is one of the lesser-known but significant incarnations of Lord Shiva, primarily mentioned in the Shiva Purana. In this form, Shiva takes on the appearance of a powerful bull (Vrishbha means bull in Sanskrit). The purpose of this avatar was to defeat the corrupt and mischievous sons of Lord Vishnu, who had grown arrogant and were causing chaos in the three worlds.

The story recounts how Lord Shiva, in the form of a majestic bull, entered the netherworld to confront and destroy these evil beings. When Lord Vishnu attempted to intervene, he eventually recognized that the mighty bull was none other than Shiva himself. This avatar symbolizes Shiva's immense strength and his role as the ultimate protector of cosmic order and righteousness. It demonstrates his willingness to take on any form to restore balance and justice when the universe is in peril.

Chapter 11: The Piplad Avatar: A Cosmic Act of Mercy

In the vast and intricate tapestry of Hindu mythology, Lord Shiva, the Mahadev, is revered as a paradox—a destroyer and a creator, a fierce ascetic and a compassionate protector. While his most famous forms, such as Nataraja and Ardhanarishvara, embody cosmic principles, his lesser-known incarnations reveal his profound and direct intervention in the affairs of the mortal and celestial realms. The **Piplad** avatar stands as a testament to this profound mercy, a form born not out of fury or pride, but from a divine act of salvation aimed at correcting a cosmic injustice. This story is a powerful narrative of righteous vengeance, boundless compassion, and the ultimate victory of devotion over the harshest of fates.

The Foundation of Injustice: The Saga of Sage Dadhichi

To truly understand the purpose of the Piplad avatar, one must first comprehend the plight of the great sage **Dadhichi**. He was an embodiment of unwavering devotion and selflessness, a sage whose very life was a continuous act of penance and sacrifice. In the cosmic order, every being, mortal or divine, is subject to the influence of the planets, particularly **Shani** (Saturn). Shani is known as the lord of karma, a powerful deity who delivers justice and consequence with unyielding discipline. His influence, particularly during the dreaded **Shani Mahadasha** (a major planetary period) and **Sade Sati** (a seven-and-a-half-year cycle), is said to be severe, bringing immense challenges, suffering, and hardship to cleanse one's karma.

For reasons known only to the divine plan, Shani's gaze was cast upon Dadhichi. Despite the sage's impeccable righteousness, he was destined to undergo the most brutal phase of Shani's influence. This was not a punishment for past misdeeds, but a preordained trial that seemed to defy the very principles of dharma. The suffering of the sage was so intense that it was believed to have a lasting impact on his future lineage, a karmic shadow that would follow his descendants. Dadhichi accepted his fate with grace, but the celestial injustice did not go unnoticed by the supreme deities. It was this seemingly unalterable decree of fate that would compel Shiva to manifest in a new form.

The Divine Birth from the Pipal Tree

From this backdrop of cosmic tribulation, a profound event occurred. Lord Shiva, moved by the injustice and suffering of his devotee, decided to intervene. He manifested a divine presence under a sacred **Pipal tree** (*Ficus religiosa*). The Pipal tree is an ancient symbol of spiritual knowledge and a dwelling place for gods, and it was from this sacred, life-giving source that Shiva's new form was born. A beautiful and radiant child, pulsating with divine energy, emerged. He was found by the sages under the tree and was named **Piplad**, a name that literally means "one who comes from the Pipal."

Piplad was not an ordinary child. He was an instant manifestation of Shiva's resolve. Raised by the wise sages, he quickly absorbed the knowledge of the cosmos and the intricacies of the divine order. His intelligence and spiritual power were extraordinary, and he soon learned of his own divine heritage and the tragic story of his father, Dadhichi, and the immense suffering inflicted upon him by Shani. The knowledge of his father's plight awakened a righteous fury within him. This was not a destructive rage, but a pure, unadulterated fire of justice. Piplad's single-minded purpose was to confront the celestial force that had brought so much sorrow to his family and to countless others.

The Righteous Vengeance: Confronting Shani

To accomplish his mission, Piplad performed a severe and unwavering penance, dedicating himself to the worship of his divine father, Shiva. His austerities were so intense that they sent ripples through the cosmos, signaling to all the planets and gods that a new power had arisen. When he had accrued sufficient spiritual power, Piplad summoned Shani.

The confrontation that followed was a clash not of physical strength, but of cosmic will. Shani, as the embodiment of justice and karma, stood firm in his duty. He explained that he was merely an instrument of fate, a tool to deliver the consequences of actions, both past and present. But Piplad countered, arguing that true justice must also be tempered with mercy. He believed that the suffering of the innocent, particularly a soul as pure as Dadhichi, was an aberration that needed to be corrected.

In a climactic moment of divine authority, Piplad used his supreme power to deliver a curse. He declared that Shani, from that moment on, would have no malefic influence over any child **under the age of 16**. This was a precise and targeted act of salvation. The curse was not to strip Shani of his power entirely, but to carve out a sacred exception, creating a period of grace and protection for the most vulnerable. Children, in their innocence and purity, would be shielded from the harshest of karmic trials, allowing them to grow, learn, and build a foundation for their lives without the heavy hand of Saturn's influence.

Realizing the immense power and righteous purpose of this new avatar, Shani humbly accepted the curse. He understood that Shiva's divine compassion was meant to restore balance, not just through destruction, but through compassionate intervention. From that day forward, the curse became a cosmic law, and Piplad became the revered protector of all children from the ill effects of Shani.

The Spiritual and Astrological Significance

The story of the Piplad avatar holds profound spiritual and astrological significance for devotees.

A Symbol of Hope and Protection: The most important lesson of this avatar is that even the most unyielding forces of fate can be mitigated by divine grace. The story provides hope to those who feel trapped by the adverse effects of planetary alignments. It teaches that through sincere devotion to Shiva, one can find a path to relief and protection. Piplad is the embodiment of Shiva's promise to his devotees: that he will always stand by them, even against the forces that govern destiny.

The Sacred Pipal Tree: The Pipal tree, from which Piplad was born, holds a special place in this mythology. It is not merely a backdrop but a sacred symbol of this incarnation. Devotees who wish to seek Piplad's protection or appease Shani often perform rituals under a Pipal tree. The very act of offering water to the roots of a Pipal tree is considered a form of worship that can alleviate the suffering caused by Shani's influence. This practice is believed to connect the devotee directly to the energy of the Piplad avatar, drawing upon his protective grace.

A Remedy for Shani's Influence: In Vedic astrology, the story of Piplad is considered one of the most powerful remedies for mitigating the effects of Shani's periods. Astrologers often recommend that individuals undergoing a difficult Shani Mahadasha or Sade Sati worship Lord Shiva and specifically venerate the Piplad form. This is particularly relevant for those who are facing difficulties that feel overwhelming or unjust. Chanting specific mantras, performing simple rituals under a Pipal tree, and seeking the blessings of Shiva as Piplad are all considered effective ways to find relief from cosmic trials.

In conclusion, the Piplad avatar is more than just a story; it is a sacred lesson in divine justice and compassion. It reminds us that Shiva is not a distant, unapproachable deity, but a vigilant protector who will manifest in any form necessary to save his devotees. Through the righteous fury of a child born from a sacred tree, he corrected a cosmic injustice, proving that love and mercy can triumph even over the unyielding laws of karma. The Piplad avatar stands as an eternal symbol of hope, a powerful reminder that even in the face of the most challenging destinies, Shiva's grace is a constant and unwavering presence.

Chapter 12: The Nandi Avatar: A Cosmic Act of Devotion

In the vast and intricate pantheon of Hindu deities, Lord Shiva is often portrayed in a state of profound contemplation, his eyes closed in eternal meditation. Yet, his presence is never solitary. By his side, in every depiction, stands his loyal vahana (mount) and chief attendant, **Nandi**, the divine bull. While often seen as merely a vehicle, Nandi is far more than that; he is a powerful and significant avatar of Shiva himself, an embodiment of dharma, justice, and the ultimate form of a devotee. The story of Nandi's birth and his subsequent elevation to his divine role is not just a tale of creation, but a profound narrative of how unwavering devotion can transform a mortal existence into an immortal one. This avatar reveals Shiva’s immense compassion for his followers and his readiness to grant supreme salvation to those who seek him with a pure heart. Nandi's purpose as a saviour is not to vanquish demons, but to guide souls to the path of righteousness and protect the divine order from all threats.

The Foundation of Devotion: The Saga of Sage Shilada

The origin of Nandi begins not with a celestial decree, but with the heartfelt desire of a mortal sage. The great ascetic **Shilada**, a staunch devotee of Lord Shiva, lived a life of rigorous penance and sacrifice. He had no desire for material wealth or worldly pleasures, but he harbored a deep yearning for a son. His wish was unique, however; he did not want an ordinary human child who would be subject to the endless cycle of birth and death. Instead, Shilada desired a son who would be immortal, blessed with divine qualities, and who would be a direct manifestation of Lord Shiva's grace. To achieve this, he undertook a formidable penance, meditating on Shiva with a single-pointed focus for thousands of years.

Shilada's unwavering devotion and immense spiritual energy resonated throughout the cosmos, reaching the ears of Lord Shiva himself. Known as a deity who is easily pleased by true devotion, Shiva appeared before the sage in all his glory, his body adorned with snakes, his hair matted, and his third eye radiating cosmic power. He smiled upon Shilada, granting his boon. Shiva told the sage that he would receive a son who was a part of Shiva himself, a divine being who would be a source of eternal joy. This promise was the first step in the creation of the Nandi avatar.

The Divine Birth and the Test of Fate

Upon returning to his hermitage, Shilada performed a grand fire sacrifice, as instructed by Shiva. From the sacred flames, a radiant and perfect child emerged, a being born not from a womb, but from the spiritual energy of Shiva's blessing. The boy shone with the brilliance of a thousand suns and was named **Nandi** by the sages, meaning "the one who brings joy." Nandi grew at an astonishing pace, and from his earliest years, he displayed an extraordinary intelligence and an innate understanding of the Vedas and spiritual knowledge. He was an embodiment of purity and wisdom, a child whose sole focus was on his father and on the worship of Shiva.

However, a crisis soon arose, one that would test Nandi's resolve and ultimately pave the way for his divine transformation. Two celestial messengers, **Mitra** and **Varuna**, visited Shilada's hermitage. After observing the child, they delivered a grim prophecy: Nandi's life would be short, destined to end before he reached the age of eight. This news devastated Shilada, who had cherished his divine son, but it did not frighten Nandi. He responded with a calm and unwavering spirit that belied his age. He reminded his father that he was born to a divine purpose and that death was merely a test of faith. This moment is crucial, for it demonstrates the very essence of the Nandi avatar: a complete and total surrender to the divine will, even in the face of mortality.

Nandi, with a resolve that would inspire all future devotees, embarked on a period of intense penance. He left his father's home and immersed himself in meditation, focusing all his energy on Lord Shiva. He practiced austerities, consuming nothing but air, and meditated with such intensity that his spiritual power surpassed that of many great sages. His body, now slender from his fasting, became a beacon of divine energy, his mind a channel for constant communion with Shiva.

The Boon of Immortality and the Divine Elevation

Moved by this profound and unwavering devotion, Lord Shiva once again appeared before Nandi. This time, he was not just a granter of boons, but a loving father, a divine protector. Shiva embraced Nandi and showered him with blessings. He granted Nandi the gift of immortality, ensuring that death would never be able to claim him. But Shiva's greatest blessing was yet to come. Recognizing Nandi's selfless love and complete surrender, Shiva anointed him as the **chief of his Ganas** (attendants), the gatekeeper of his divine abode, **Mount Kailash**, and his personal vahana, or mount. Nandi was now a direct extension of Shiva's will, a part of the divine family. He was adorned with a beautiful garland of bells and given a place of honor right beside the Lord. The Nandi avatar was complete.

Nandi as a Protector and Gatekeeper

Nandi's role as an avatar of Shiva is most powerfully demonstrated in his function as a protector. He is not a warrior in the traditional sense, but his presence alone is enough to deter any threat. He is the guardian of the sanctum sanctorum, the silent and vigilant sentinel at the entrance of Shiva's sacred space. The most famous story illustrating this is his encounter with the arrogant demon king, **Ravana**.

Ravana, with his unmatched strength and pride, sought to conquer Mount Kailash itself. He believed his power was supreme and that he could easily uproot the very mountain where Shiva resided. As he approached the sacred peak, he was confronted by Nandi. Nandi warned him to retreat, as Mount Kailash was not a mountain to be trifled with, and Shiva was in deep meditation. Ravana, in his arrogance, dismissed the words of the divine bull and laughed mockingly. Infuriated by the demon's disrespect, Nandi, in a flash of divine fury, cursed him. He prophesied that Ravana's downfall would be brought about by a common monkey, a curse that would later come to fruition in the form of Lord Hanuman. The curse was a direct result of Nandi's function as a protector of dharma and the divine abode. When Ravana, in his hubris, began to shake the mountain, Shiva, with a simple press of his toe, pinned him beneath it, trapping him for thousands of years. Nandi's curse was a precursor to this divine punishment, a manifestation of Shiva's protective will.

Nandi as a Conveyor of Knowledge

Beyond his protective duties, Nandi also functions as a divine teacher and the first to receive Shiva's wisdom. As Shiva's most trusted attendant, he is privy to the most profound spiritual knowledge. It is said that Shiva whispers the secrets of the cosmos to Nandi, who in turn relays them to the sages and seers. Nandi is the primordial source of much of the knowledge of the **Agamas**, ancient texts that detail the rituals and philosophy of Shaivism. His role as a teacher is a central aspect of his avatar, positioning him as a link between the formless reality of

Shiva and the mortal world seeking enlightenment. This is a crucial function of a saviour: to not just protect, but to also guide souls to liberation by imparting the knowledge necessary for their spiritual journey.

Furthermore, Nandi's role in the celestial dance, the **Tandava**, is paramount. He is not merely an audience but a participant, a cosmic witness to Shiva's creative and destructive dance. It is Nandi who first grasps the rhythm and the profound meaning of the Tandava, and he is the one who inspires the sages to understand its spiritual significance.

Nandi as a Vindicator of Justice

Another key aspect of the Nandi avatar is his role as a vindicator of justice. He is a bull of unshakeable loyalty, and any disrespect shown to his master is met with a swift and righteous response. The most famous example of this is the **Daksha Yagna**. When the arrogant king **Daksha**, Shiva's father-in-law, insulted Shiva and excluded him from a great sacrifice, all the gods and sages who attended the yagna showed disrespect by not standing up for the Lord. Nandi, who was present, could not tolerate this blatant injustice. In a fit of righteous rage, he cursed all the deities who had remained silent. He cursed Brahma to be worshipped by only a few, cursed Indra to lose his kingdom, and cursed all those who supported Daksha's yagna to suffer from Shiva's wrath. This curse, delivered with the full authority of a divine avatar, demonstrated that Nandi was not a passive attendant, but an active participant in upholding the cosmic order.

The Enduring Symbolism of Nandi

The Nandi avatar holds deep symbolic meaning for every Hindu, and his image is a staple at the entrance of every Shiva temple.

The Bull of Dharma: Nandi is most famously depicted as a bull, the ancient symbol of **dharma**, or righteousness. Just as a bull is strong, steadfast, and unyielding, so too must the path of dharma be. Nandi's presence at the temple's entrance signifies that one must possess the qualities of righteousness, purity, and unwavering devotion to enter the divine space. His four legs are often said to represent the four virtues of a perfect devotee: truth, purity, compassion, and dharma.

The Eternal Devotee: Nandi is the ultimate representation of a devotee. He sits eternally, with his gaze fixed upon the divine sanctum, a silent lesson in total concentration and surrender. His story teaches that the path to liberation is not a journey of grand acts, but one of sincere devotion, humility, and unwavering faith. The very act of whispering one's prayers into Nandi's ear before entering the temple is a common practice, born from the belief that Nandi, as Shiva's closest confidante, will relay the prayers directly to the Lord.

The Guardian of the Self: On a deeper spiritual level, Nandi represents the guardian of the self. Before one can achieve a union with the divine (Shiva), one must first control their own ego and senses, symbolized by the bull's fierce yet disciplined nature. Nandi is the gatekeeper of the inner sanctum, reminding us that true worship begins not with external rituals, but with internal purification.

In conclusion, the Nandi avatar is a powerful and multifaceted manifestation of Lord Shiva. He is a saviour in the truest sense of the word—not just a vanquisher of physical demons, but a protector of cosmic order, a conveyor of divine wisdom, and a living testament to the transformative power of devotion. His story provides a timeless guide for all spiritual aspirants, showing that a life dedicated to the divine, no matter how humble its beginnings, can lead to the highest state of consciousness and eternal bliss. Nandi's silent, patient presence at the door of every Shiva temple is a constant reminder that the path to liberation is open to all who have the courage to walk it with a pure heart.

Chapter 13: The Virabhadra Avatar: The Cosmic Manifestation of Wrath

In the complex and multidimensional world of Hindu mythology, Lord Shiva, the Mahadev, embodies both destruction and creation, a tranquil ascetic and a fearsome warrior. Of his many avatars, none is as potent and terrifying as **Virabhadra**, a form born not from calm contemplation, but from a cataclysmic surge of divine grief and rage. This incarnation is not a saviour in the traditional sense of protecting the innocent, but a vindicator of cosmic justice, a force of nature summoned to punish arrogance and restore balance. The story of Virabhadra's creation is a powerful and emotional narrative that stands as a foundational myth in Shaivism and a testament to the profound consequences of disrespecting the divine.

The Genesis of Wrath: The Saga of Daksha and Sati

The story of Virabhadra is inseparable from the tragic tale of **Sati**, the youngest daughter of King **Daksha Prajapati**. Daksha was a proud and powerful king who held a deep-seated animosity towards Shiva. Despite his daughter's unwavering devotion to the ascetic god, Daksha viewed Shiva as an unconventional and ill-mannered deity, unworthy of his daughter's hand. He despised Shiva's simple lifestyle, his matted hair, and his association with cremation grounds and spirits. Sati, however, had chosen

Shiva as her husband against her father's wishes. This act of defiance only fueled Daksha's hatred.

Daksha's animosity came to a head when he decided to perform a grand **Yagna** (ritual fire sacrifice). He invited all the gods, sages, and celestial beings, but deliberately and publicly omitted Shiva and Sati from the guest list. This was a direct and grave insult, a deliberate act of public humiliation designed to undermine Shiva's status and authority. The gods and other attendees, though they knew of Daksha's injustice, remained silent, too fearful of his power to speak out.

Sati, her heart torn between her father and her husband, insisted on attending the Yagna, believing she could mediate the conflict. Shiva, in his infinite wisdom, warned her against it, stating that one should never go to an uninvited ceremony, as it leads to dishonor. However, Sati, driven by her love for her family and her husband, ignored his advice and went to the Yagna alone. Upon her arrival, Daksha launched into a tirade of insults, publicly mocking Shiva in front of the entire assembly. He called Shiva a deranged ascetic, a "bhuta-natha" (lord of ghosts), and a disgrace to the divine order. Unable to bear the humiliation and disrespect towards her beloved husband, Sati, consumed by rage and grief, used her yogic power to immolate herself in the sacrificial fire.

The Emergence of Virabhadra: A Form of Unbridled Fury

When the news of Sati's self-immolation reached Shiva, his grief was beyond comprehension, and his rage was boundless. His serene, meditative state was shattered, replaced by a cosmic fury that threatened to unravel the very fabric of the universe. In a moment of supreme anguish, Shiva tore a clump of his matted hair (**Jata**) and hurled it to the ground. From this single lock of hair, a monstrous and terrifying warrior was born, a being of unimaginable power and ferocity. This was **Virabhadra**.

Virabhadra's appearance was a direct reflection of Shiva's rage. He was described as having a terrifying form, reaching the heavens with his stature, and having a complexion as dark as a storm cloud. He had a thousand arms, each one holding a different weapon of destruction—swords, tridents, bows, and clubs. His hair was like fire, his eyes blazed with fury, and he wore a garland of skulls. His very presence radiated a power that instilled fear in even the mightiest of gods. Along with Virabhadra, a fierce goddess named **Bhadrakali** was also born from Shiva's rage, serving as his female counterpart in the quest for vengeance.

The Vengeance: Upholding Cosmic Justice

Shiva, with a voice that echoed throughout the cosmos, commanded Virabhadra to destroy the Yagna, to punish all those who had remained silent in the face of injustice, and to sever the head of Daksha. Accompanied by Bhadrakali and his hordes of Ganas, Virabhadra stormed the ceremonial grounds. What followed was a scene of utter chaos and destruction.

The gods and sages, who had previously been so arrogant and complacent, fled in terror. Virabhadra, with his boundless strength, laid waste to the entire assembly. He beheaded Daksha in a single, swift motion. The celestial beings who had attended the Yagna did not escape his wrath. Virabhadra broke the limbs of Agni, the god of fire; plucked out the eyes of Bhaga, the sun god; and broke the teeth of Pushan. The entire cosmic order was thrown into disarray as Virabhadra's fury was a force that no one, not even the Trimurti (Brahma, Vishnu, and Shiva) could contain.

The gods, humbled and terrified, appealed to Shiva to calm his avatar and restore the balance. Shiva, seeing the devastation wrought by his own grief, eventually pacified Virabhadra. He then took his most compassionate form to heal the wounds. He restored Daksha's life, but instead of his original head, he gave him the head of a goat, a lasting symbol of his arrogance and humiliation. This act was a powerful lesson in cosmic justice: the punishment was severe, but it was also tempered with mercy, allowing for a new beginning.

The Significance of the Avatar

The Virabhadra avatar holds a deep and multifaceted significance for devotees and spiritual seekers.

The Wrath of the Righteous: Virabhadra represents the principle that while patience and forgiveness are divine qualities, there are moments when righteous anger is necessary to restore balance. His destructive act was not born of malice, but of a fierce commitment to justice. He embodies the principle that when dharma is violated, a force must rise to correct it. This avatar serves as a warning against arrogance, pride, and disrespect towards the divine.

The Ultimate Protector: While Virabhadra's actions were destructive, his ultimate purpose was protective. He was created to defend Shiva's honor and to ensure that no one would ever again dare to insult the supreme deity. He is the guardian who stands ready to destroy the forces of evil and arrogance, acting as a divine saviour for those who follow the path of righteousness.

A Metaphor for Spiritual Transformation: On a deeper, more spiritual level, the story of Daksha's Yagna and Virabhadra's vengeance is a powerful metaphor for the internal spiritual journey. In this interpretation, **Daksha** represents the ego and arrogance of the individual. **Sati** symbolizes a pure and devoted heart, and **Shiva** is the supreme consciousness. The Yagna is the stage of worldly desires and attachments that the ego uses to assert its dominance. Virabhadra, therefore, is the force that we must summon within ourselves to destroy our own ego, pride, and ignorance in order to achieve true spiritual liberation. His destructive power is not an end in itself, but a necessary force for internal cleansing, a brutal but compassionate act that allows the soul to connect with the divine.

Chapter 14: The Fierce Guardian of Time: An Exploration of the Bhairava Avatar of Lord Shiva

In the vast and complex pantheon of Hindu deities, few figures command as much awe and reverence as Lord Shiva. He is the ultimate paradox: the destroyer and the creator, the ascetic and the householder, the fierce and the tranquil. Among his most formidable and fascinating manifestations is Bhairava, a form so terrifying and powerful that his name alone evokes a profound sense of cosmic authority. Bhairava, meaning "the terrifying" or "the fearsome," is not merely a wrathful aspect of Shiva; he is the very embodiment of time, the ultimate reality, and the supreme guardian who stands at the threshold of creation and dissolution. His presence is a stark reminder that true divinity encompasses not only the serene and beautiful but also the wild, untamed, and relentless forces of the universe.

The Myth of Origin: The Beheading of Brahma

The most prominent and widely recounted myth of Bhairava's origin is found in the *Shiva Purana.* This story serves to establish Bhairava's cosmic role and to explain his fierce iconography. The tale begins with a dispute between Lord Vishnu, the preserver, and Lord Brahma, the creator, over who was the supreme deity in the cosmos. Brahma, filled with arrogance and a sense of superiority, proclaimed himself the ultimate creator and even went so far as to claim he had five heads, just like Shiva, making him equal in power. He began to interfere with Shiva's duties and to treat him with disrespect.

Shiva, witnessing Brahma's ego and falsehood, remained silent for a time. However, when Brahma's hubris became unbearable, Shiva manifested a fierce, terrifying form from a mere nail on his finger. This being, dark-complexioned and fearsome, was Bhairava. Bhairava sought instruction from his creator, Shiva, who commanded him to punish Brahma for his arrogance and dishonesty. Without hesitation, Bhairava advanced upon Brahma and, with a swift stroke of his sword, severed the fifth head of the creator god. The act instantly humbled Brahma, reducing him to his original form with only four heads, and re-established Shiva as the supreme reality.

However, the sin of *Brahmahatya*—the heinous crime of killing a Brahmin—instantly clung to Bhairava. In Hindu mythology, Brahma is the first Brahmin, and the act of beheading him, even if he was in the wrong, had karmic consequences. Brahma's severed head became a skull that fused to Bhairava's left hand, serving as a constant reminder of his sin. To atone, Bhairava was condemned to wander the three worlds as a naked ascetic (*Digambara*), carrying the skull as his begging bowl, a form known as *Kapalika*. His penance led him on a long pilgrimage, during which he was relentlessly pursued by the personification of the sin, a terrifying entity known as Brahmahatya. His liberation came only when he reached the holy city of Varanasi (Kashi), a place where the sin of Brahmahatya cannot follow. Upon entering Kashi, the skull fell from his hand, and he was finally absolved. Because of this legend, Bhairava is venerated as the *Kotwal* (guardian) of Kashi, and it is said that no one can enter the city without his permission.

The Symbolism of Bhairava's Iconography

Bhairava's physical form is rich with symbolic meaning, each element revealing a deeper truth about his nature. He is typically depicted with a dark complexion, often described as blue or black, symbolizing his association with the transcendent, formless reality that exists beyond all manifestation. His bulging, terrifying eyes and sharp fangs convey his fierce nature, but this is not a sign of malice; it is the righteous anger directed at the forces of ignorance and ego.

He is often shown wearing a garland of skulls, representing the skulls of ego and attachment that he helps his devotees to shed. His sacred thread, instead of being made of cotton, is a snake, symbolizing the Kundalini energy he masters. Bhairava's four hands hold a variety of powerful implements: a trident, which represents the three fundamental energies of creation, preservation, and destruction; a noose, for binding and removing obstacles; a drum (*damaru*), symbolizing the cosmic rhythm of creation; and the severed head of Brahma as his begging bowl.

The most iconic aspect of his iconography is the dog (*shvan*), which is his divine vehicle (*vahana*). The dog is often seen as a symbol of loyalty, but in the context of

Bhairava, it also represents a fierce and protective instinct. The dog is an unyielding guardian, and in the same way, Bhairava protects his devotees from harm and guides them on the spiritual path. This relationship between the fierce deity and his faithful companion underscores Bhairava's role as both a terrifying punisher and a compassionate protector.

The Eight Bhairavas (Ashtabhairava)

Beyond his primary form, Bhairava manifests in a multitude of aspects, each with a specific function and symbolism. The most prominent are the eight **Ashtabhairavas**, who are believed to guard and control the eight cardinal directions. Each of these forms is associated with a specific consort (*Shakti*), a vehicle, and a unique set of attributes. Collectively, they represent the multifaceted nature of divine power and the mastery over all aspects of the universe.

1. **Asitanga Bhairava (East):** With a white complexion, he is the embodiment of creation. He is associated with knowledge, creativity, and the arts, and his vehicle is a swan.
2. **Ruru Bhairava (Southeast):** Light blue in color, Ruru is the guardian of knowledge and wisdom. He rides a bull and inspires intellectual growth and spiritual inquiry.
3. **Chanda Bhairava (South):** White-complexioned, he personifies strength and valor. His vehicle is a peacock, and he is

worshipped for courage and protection against enemies.

4. **Krodha Bhairava (Southwest):** Dark blue, Krodha embodies righteous anger and justice. He rides an eagle and is invoked to overcome negative influences and ensure justice prevails.
5. **Unmatta Bhairava (West):** Golden-complexioned, Unmatta represents a state of ecstatic bliss and freedom from illusion. His vehicle is a horse, and he helps devotees control their negative traits.
6. **Kapala Bhairava (Northwest):** Shining yellow in color, Kapala symbolizes the fruits of one's efforts. He rides an elephant and is worshipped to ensure successful completion of endeavors and to end delays.
7. **Bhishana Bhairava (North):** Blood-red, Bhishana is the remover of fear and the destroyer of evil spirits. His vehicle is a lion, and he provides protection from negative energies and instills a sense of fearlessness.
8. **Samhara Bhairava (Northeast):** Lightning-yellow-orange, Samhara is the fierce annihilator who helps devotees shed their bad karma and start a new, spiritual life. He rides a lion and is a bringer of radical transformation.

These eight forms further subdivide into 64 Bhairavas, each governing a different realm of existence and working in conjunction with 64 Yoginis. This complex system of divine hierarchies underscores Bhairava's pervasive and all-encompassing power over the entire cosmic order.

The Cosmic Significance: Bhairava as Kala and Kshetrapala

The title *Kala Bhairava* is perhaps his most significant. *Kala* literally means "time," but it also refers to "death" or "fate." Bhairava is the lord of time, and in this role, he is both the master and the destroyer of it. He is a reminder that everything in the material world is subject to the passage of time and its inevitable conclusion—death. However, Bhairava himself stands beyond time, and by worshipping him, devotees seek to transcend the fear of death and attain liberation (*moksha*). He is the ultimate reality that remains after the cosmic dissolution, standing as the eternal, unchanging consciousness.

In his role as *Kshetrapala*, Bhairava is the "protector of the field." This title has a literal and a spiritual meaning. In a literal sense, he is the guardian of all temples, especially those dedicated to Shiva. In many Shiva temples across India, Bhairava's shrine is placed near the entrance, and it is customary for devotees to seek his blessings before entering the main sanctum. Spiritually, he is the guardian of the sacred space of the human body, protecting the devotee from both internal and external negative forces. His fierce form is a shield, warding off obstacles, malevolent spirits, and internal enemies like ego, greed, and anger.

Bhairava in Worship and Tantra

Bhairava's worship is particularly prevalent in the Shaiva tradition, especially in its more esoteric and tantric forms. Unlike other deities who are worshipped with gentle rituals, Bhairava's veneration often involves more intense practices. He is the principal deity of the Aghora sect, known for its extreme and non-conventional spiritual practices that seek to transcend all worldly dualities, including purity and impurity, fear and courage.

The most common day for Bhairava worship is Sunday, particularly during the *Ashtami* lunar phase, which is considered highly auspicious. Traditional offerings include black sesame seeds, mustard oil, and sometimes even liquor, symbolizing the breaking of societal norms and the offering of that which is considered profane to a deity who transcends all such distinctions. The act of offering to Bhairava is believed to cleanse the devotee of their sins and to grant them protection. Feeding street dogs is also a significant ritual, as they are considered his sacred vehicles.

Reciting the *Kala Bhairava Ashtakam*, a hymn of eight stanzas dedicated to him, is considered a powerful way to invoke his blessings and to gain courage, wisdom, and protection. The chant is said to bring clarity to the mind and help in overcoming the fear of death.

The Compassionate Fear

While Bhairava's appearance is terrifying, his nature is deeply compassionate. His wrath is not that of a malevolent being but of a loving father who is firm in his discipline. He destroys not to cause suffering but to liberate. He instills fear in the wicked and the ignorant to protect the righteous. His fierce form serves as a powerful instrument to cut through our delusions and attachments, forcing us to confront our inner demons and to realize the ultimate, fearless nature of the soul.

In conclusion, the Bhairava avatar of Lord Shiva is a profound and multi-layered aspect of the supreme being. He is the primordial force that stands at the very edge of time, the fierce guardian who protects the cosmos and its devotees, and the compassionate master who guides us toward liberation by helping us confront our greatest fears. His story is not just a mythological tale but a spiritual lesson about the necessity of transformation through destruction, the mastery over time, and the ultimate victory of the self over its own illusions. His fearsome exterior conceals a truth of absolute protection and unwavering grace for those who surrender to his divine power.

Chapter 15: The Sharabha Avatar: The Embodiment of Cosmic Balance

In the vast and intricate tapestry of Hindu mythology, where gods and demons engage in cosmic dances of creation and destruction, a profound tale unfolds concerning the Sharabha avatar of Lord Shiva. This is not a story of conquest, but of restoration—a powerful narrative that illuminates the delicate balance of the universe and the ultimate harmony between its supreme deities.

The saga begins in the wake of Lord Vishnu's dramatic appearance as Narasimha, the man-lion. Born from a pillar to protect his devotee Prahlada, Narasimha's ferocity knew no bounds as he annihilated the demon king Hiranyakashipu. However, even after the demon's demise, the divine rage of Narasimha did not subside. His roars shook the heavens, his claws dripped with cosmic energy, and his wrath threatened to consume the very foundations of the three worlds. The Devas, trembling with fear, found themselves helpless before this raw, untamed force. They prayed to the Trimurti, seeking a solution to this unprecedented crisis.

In that moment of cosmic peril, Lord Shiva, the great ascetic and destroyer, responded to their pleas. Understanding that only a force of equal, if not greater, magnitude could contain Narasimha's fury, Shiva manifested as Sharabha. The Sharabha avatar is a magnificent and awe-inspiring being, a creature of cosmic design. He possesses the body of a lion, symbolizing unparalleled strength, but with a bird's head and a pair of massive, feathered wings that allowed him to soar across the cosmos. He is depicted with eight legs, signifying his mastery over all directions, and with four arms holding weapons of immense power. This form, part lion and part bird, was a living paradox—a fusion of earth's might and the heavens' freedom, a testament to Shiva's ability to transcend all known forms to restore order.

The confrontation between Sharabha and Narasimha was an event of unparalleled grandeur. The clash was not born of animosity but of a sacred duty to restore cosmic equilibrium. Sharabha met Narasimha's roars with a cry of his own, and their battle became a spectacle of pure divine power. The universe watched in bated breath as the two supreme beings engaged in combat. Sharabha's immense strength and agility were perfectly matched against Narasimha's uncontrollable rage. With each maneuver, Sharabha sought not to destroy, but to contain, to absorb the wild energy. Finally, through a series of powerful and precise blows, Sharabha managed to subdue Narasimha. He held the man-lion in a firm embrace, and as the fury was siphoned from Narasimha's body, he transformed back into his tranquil, four-armed form as Lord Vishnu.

The significance of Sharabha Bhagwan extends far beyond this single mythological event. He is revered as the ultimate embodiment of control, a divine figure who can pacify even the most formidable forces. This narrative serves as a profound theological statement on the harmony between Shiva and Vishnu, often seen as rival deities in simpler tales. The Sharabha Purana and other Puranic texts highlight that Shiva's intervention was an act of profound respect and affection for Vishnu, underscoring their shared role in maintaining cosmic balance. Sharabha is a powerful symbol that illustrates how even the most destructive energies can be tamed and integrated back into the harmonious flow of existence. He reminds us that true power lies not in unchecked force, but in the wisdom to know when to use it to bring forth peace and order.

Chapter 16: The Grihapati Avatar - The Divine Householder

The vast and intricate tapestry of Hindu mythology is woven with countless tales of gods and goddesses, each manifesting in various forms to restore cosmic balance, protect their devotees, or impart profound spiritual lessons. While the fierce forms of Lord Shiva, such as Bhairava and Veerabhadra, are widely known for their power and wrath, a quieter, more compassionate avatar exists, one that speaks directly to the heart of human existence and the sanctity of the family. This is the Grihapati avatar, the divine householder, a form that beautifully illustrates how spirituality is not confined to asceticism in remote forests but can flourish within the walls of a home, blessed by love, devotion, and a deep connection to the divine.

The story of Grihapati is a rare gem, primarily found within the Shiva Purana, specifically in the Shatarudra Samhita. It is a tale that begins not with a cataclysmic battle or a cosmic crisis, but with the simple, yet profound, desire of a pious couple for a child. On the banks of the sacred Narmada River lived a devout Brahmin named Visvanara and his virtuous wife, Shuchismati. They led a righteous life, dedicated to their spiritual duties and household responsibilities, but a deep sorrow lingered in their hearts: they were childless. Shuchismati, longing for a son, expressed her heartfelt desire to her husband, wishing for a child who would be the very embodiment of Lord Shiva himself.

Moved by his wife's unwavering faith and her divine wish, Visvanara resolved to undertake a rigorous penance to please Lord Shiva. He journeyed to the holy city of Kashi (modern-day Varanasi), a city believed to be Shiva's eternal abode. In Kashi, he found a sacred spot and began his austere worship of the Vishweshwara Linga. For months, he performed his penance with unparalleled devotion, restricting his food and water, his mind fixed solely on the image of Mahadeva. So profound was his dedication that it moved the heavens. Lord Shiva, pleased beyond measure, manifested before him not in his terrifying form, but as a small, radiant boy emerging from the very Linga Visvanara worshipped.

Recognizing the divine presence, Visvanara fell to his knees in reverence and offered eulogies. Lord Shiva, in his playful and compassionate nature, then took the form of an old man and granted Visvanara his boon: he would be born as their son. Overjoyed, Visvanara returned to his hermitage, his heart overflowing with gratitude. In due course, Shuchismati gave birth to a beautiful and effulgent child, a divine incarnation of Lord Shiva himself. The birth was celebrated by all the deities and sages, including Lord Brahma and Goddess Parvati, who arrived to bless the infant. Lord Brahma, recognizing the child's purpose and destiny as a householder, named him Grihapati, meaning "the lord of the house" or "the master of the home."

The young Grihapati grew with astonishing speed, displaying an incredible intellect and spiritual inclination from a very young age. His sacred thread ceremony was performed when he was just five years old, and within a year, he had mastered all the Vedas and other sacred texts. His knowledge was profound, his devotion unshakeable, and his presence brought immense joy and blessings to his parents. Yet, the divine play was not without its challenges.

When Grihapati reached the age of nine, the wandering sage Narada, known for his ability to see into the past, present, and future, visited their home. Upon examining Grihapati's astrological chart, Narada delivered a grave and unsettling prophecy: due to malefic planetary combinations, Grihapati was destined to meet his end from a fire or lightning bolt. Visvanara and Shuchismati were devastated, their joy turning into unbearable sorrow. They wept bitterly, unable to comprehend why their divine son, whom they had received through such hardship, was fated for such a tragic end.

Grihapati, however, remained calm and composed. He was no ordinary child; he was Shiva himself. He consoled his distraught parents, assuring them that destiny could be changed through sincere devotion and penance. He declared that he would go to Kashi to propitiate Lord Shiva and conquer his fate. His parents, though heartbroken, understood his resolve and gave him their blessings.

Upon arriving in Kashi, Grihapati found a tranquil and auspicious spot. He consecrated a Shiva Linga and began his severe penance. His devotion was so absolute that he seemed to transcend his physical body, his mind completely absorbed in meditation. It was at this point that Indra, the king of the gods, noticed the young boy's immense tapasya (penance). Indra, known for his pride and insecurity, felt his position threatened by the boy's spiritual power. He decided to test Grihapati's resolve.

Indra appeared before Grihapati and, in a condescending manner, offered him any boon he desired. Grihapati, without even opening his eyes, respectfully declined, stating that he would not accept a boon from anyone other than Lord Shiva, his ultimate refuge and the one he was performing penance for. This refusal enraged Indra, who saw it as an affront to his authority. Furious, he lifted his divine weapon, the Vajra (thunderbolt), and prepared to strike the boy.

At that very instant, a deafening sound resonated through the cosmos, and the earth trembled. The Shiva Linga that Grihapati was worshipping split open, and a glorious form of Shiva emerged. He appeared in all his ferocious majesty, ready to annihilate Indra for his arrogance. Upon seeing Mahadeva in his full glory, Indra was struck with fear and immediately dropped his Vajra, retreating from the scene in shame.

Lord Shiva then blessed Grihapati, who had remained steadfast in his devotion even in the face of death. He declared, "O Grihapati, do not fear this Vajra of Indra. From this day, not even the celestial thunderbolt or the thunder of Kaalavajra will be able to harm you." He granted him the boon of being the lord of all directions and the presiding deity of all fire rituals. The Shiva Linga that Grihapati had worshipped became famous as the Agnishwar Linga, the "Linga of the Lord of Fire," a testament to his divine connection with the element of Agni.

The significance of the Grihapati avatar extends far beyond this particular narrative. It is a profound spiritual lesson for all of humanity.

Firstly, the Grihapati avatar underscores the belief that true devotion is more powerful than destiny itself. Grihapati was fated for an early death, but his unwavering faith and sincere penance completely altered his fate. This story provides immense hope and comfort, teaching that while we cannot always control the circumstances of our lives, we can always choose our response through faith and spiritual practice. It demonstrates that a deep connection to the divine can overcome even the most formidable challenges, including the forces of fate and karma.

Secondly, this avatar beautifully reconciles the paths of a householder (Grihastha) and a spiritual seeker (Sannyasi). In ancient Vedic and Puranic traditions, the Grihastha Ashrama, or the householder stage of life, is considered the most foundational and important. It is the stage where one fulfills their duties to family and society. Grihapati's story highlights that one does not need to renounce the world to attain spiritual liberation. By living a life of devotion, righteousness, and dharma within the family, one can achieve the highest spiritual goals. This is why Shiva, the ultimate ascetic and renunciate, chose to be born as Grihapati, the divine householder. He showed that the home, with its rituals, relationships, and responsibilities, can be a sacred space for spiritual evolution.

Thirdly, the avatar establishes a deep connection between Lord Shiva and the element of fire, Agni. Grihapati, who was fated to be killed by fire, was instead transformed into its very lord. This symbolizes a spiritual alchemy: what is perceived as a threat can be transformed into a source of power and blessing through divine grace. This is why in many rituals and yajnas, Shiva is invoked as Agnishwar, the lord of fire, who purifies and sanctifies.

In conclusion, the Grihapati avatar is a beautiful and inspiring manifestation of Lord Shiva's compassion and wisdom. It is a reminder that the path to the divine is not a singular one. Whether one is a renunciate meditating in the mountains or a householder raising a family, the divine is accessible through genuine love, unwavering faith, and sincere devotion. Grihapati's journey from a fated boy to a divine protector of homes and rituals serves as a timeless guide, proving that the greatest spiritual victories are often won not on the battlefield, but in the quiet, sacred sanctuary of the human heart and home. The story invites every individual to see their own home as a temple, their family life as a form of worship, and their daily duties as a path to liberation.

The Grihapati avatar remains a powerful testament to the boundless compassion of Lord Shiva and the universal truth that the divine resides everywhere, from the grandest cosmic stage to the most humble abode. It inspires us to find our own divine purpose within the roles we play and to recognize that true spirituality is about integrating the sacred into the very fabric of our everyday lives. It is the ultimate message of Shiva, the ascetic, showing his ultimate grace as the divine householder.

Chapter 17: The Yatinath Avatar - The Sage-God and the Hunter

In the boundless and intricate mythology of Hinduism, the divine manifestations of Lord Shiva are as diverse as the cosmos itself. From the fierce fury of Veerabhadra, born to destroy arrogance, to the serene tranquility of Dakshinamurthy, the divine teacher, each avatar reveals a unique facet of the Supreme Being. Yet, among these countless forms, one avatar stands apart for its quiet and profound lesson, a testament to the idea that spiritual enlightenment is not limited to mountain caves and secluded monasteries. This is the Yatinath avatar, a form Shiva took to illustrate the power of hospitality, unwavering faith, and the possibility of achieving the highest spiritual state while living a life as a householder. This narrative, a hidden gem within the vast Puranic literature, centers on a humble hunter couple and their transformative encounter with the divine.

The story begins in the dense, ancient forests of the Vindhya mountains. There lived a skilled hunter named Aayushmat and his devoted wife, Ahalya. Their life was one of simple existence, governed by the rhythm of nature and the pursuit of sustenance. While they were not ascetics or scholars, their hearts were pure, and their devotion to Lord Shiva was absolute. Aayushmat, before every hunt, would offer prayers to Mahadeva, seeking his blessing for a successful and safe endeavor. Ahalya, in her domestic duties, would constantly chant the sacred names of Shiva, her every action a silent prayer. Their home, though a humble hut in the wilderness, was a sanctuary of piety and love, a beacon of true devotion.

One day, as the sun began its descent below the horizon, Aayushmat returned to his hut, exhausted from a long and difficult hunt. He had been unsuccessful, and his family was in need of food. Just as he was about to enter his home, he saw a guest standing at his doorstep—a tall, emaciated sage, a Yatinath, with a radiant aura and a serene, detached expression. He was a wandering ascetic, dressed in simple robes, his body smeared with sacred ash, and his eyes reflecting a deep spiritual wisdom. Aayushmat's heart swelled with reverence. According to the ancient scriptures and the very essence of their culture, a guest, especially a sage, is considered a manifestation of the divine, a living god. To serve a guest is to serve the Lord himself.

Forgetting his own hunger and fatigue, Aayushmat prostrated himself before the sage. Ahalya, seeing the divine guest, immediately joined her husband in offering the most heartfelt hospitality. They offered the sage a seat, washed his feet, and began to prepare a meal. The sage, however, was not there to simply receive their hospitality; he was there to test the depth of their devotion.

The sage, Yatinath, declared that he was famished and required a meal, but his needs were particular. He requested a meal prepared with meat from the hunt—a hunt that Aayushmat had just returned from, empty-handed. Aayushmat, without a moment's hesitation, took his bow and arrows and prepared to re-enter the perilous forest in the dead of night. Ahalya, her faith equally unshakeable, bid her husband farewell with prayers on her lips. They did not question the sage's seemingly impossible request; they simply saw it as an opportunity to serve a divine guest. Aayushmat's determination was not born of desperation, but of pure faith. He believed that if his guest's request was truly meant to be fulfilled, Shiva would guide him. And so he did. Aayushmat returned with a successful hunt, and Ahalya prepared the meal as requested.

The first test was passed, but the trial had only just begun. After partaking in the meal, the sage turned to Aayushmat with another strange and demanding request. He declared that he was still in need of comfort and wished for Ahalya to serve as his companion for the night. Ahalya was the embodiment of virtue and fidelity, and this request was a direct challenge to her chastity, the very foundation of her dharma as a wife. Aayushmat and Ahalya were momentarily stunned, their hearts heavy with the weight of the impossible choice. To deny the guest was a grave sin, a violation of the sacred duty of hospitality. To agree was to violate their marital vows and Ahalya's sacred purity.

Yet, Aayushmat's faith did not waver. He turned to his wife and, with tears in his eyes, declared that the word of a guest was paramount. The divine would not ask for anything that would truly harm them. Ahalya, in turn, demonstrated her own profound wisdom and spiritual strength. She agreed to the sage's request, but with one condition, a condition that revealed her incredible spiritual purity. She placed a single piece of cotton between herself and the sage, declaring that her body was merely an instrument of service, but her mind and soul belonged solely to her husband and to Shiva. With this act, she showed that true chastity resided not in the physical body, but in the purity of intention and mind.

This act of selfless service, of complete surrender to the divine will even in the face of what appeared to be a violation of their most sacred principles, was the final and ultimate test. The couple's faith was not blind; it was a profound trust in the divine order and in the belief that God would never truly lead them astray. Their devotion was not just a ritual, but a lived reality, a force so potent that it could overcome the most difficult of dilemmas.

As the night progressed, a brilliant light filled the small hut. The sage, Yatinath, cast off his mortal guise and revealed his true, magnificent form—the cosmic being, Lord Shiva, stood before them. His body was radiant, his third eye a symbol of divine knowledge, and his very presence filled the hut with an overwhelming sense of peace and divine bliss. The couple, stunned and overjoyed, fell at his feet, their hearts overflowing with gratitude. They had passed the ultimate test, not by doing what was easy, but by doing what was right in the face of immense adversity.

Lord Shiva, in his infinite compassion, smiled upon them and offered them a boon. Without hesitation, Aayushmat and Ahalya asked for one thing and one thing alone: liberation from the cycle of birth and death, Moksha. Lord

Shiva granted their wish and imparted a profound spiritual lesson. He told them that their life as householders, their love, their duties, and their unwavering faith were a form of penance more potent than any practiced in solitude. He revealed that true asceticism is not the rejection of the world, but the ability to live within it without attachment. The Yatinath avatar demonstrated that a home can be a hermitage, a family can be a spiritual congregation, and every act of selfless service is a direct worship of the divine.

The hunter and his wife, through their devotion to their guest, had not only been blessed by the Lord but had transcended the very need for such blessings. They had served God in his most subtle form, and in doing so, they had achieved the ultimate spiritual victory. The Yatinath avatar of Lord Shiva is a powerful reminder that the path to divinity is not reserved for the chosen few. It is open to all who have a pure heart, a steadfast mind, and a willingness to serve others without expectation. It teaches us that every home can be a temple, every family a place of worship, and every act of kindness a sacred offering to the divine. This avatar is a testament to the universal truth that the divine is found not just in grand cosmic events, but in the quiet, simple, and profound acts of human love and devotion.

Chapter 18: Sureshwar - The Lord Who Humbled the Gods

Among the countless divine manifestations of Lord Shiva, a figure of serene and subtle power exists, known to a select few as the **Sureshwar** avatar. While not as widely celebrated as the fierce Virabhadra or the all-consuming Kalabhairava, Sureshwar represents a profound and essential aspect of Shiva's divine nature: his role as the ultimate guide and teacher, one who humbles the arrogant and reminds even the mightiest gods of the supreme power that governs the cosmos. This incarnation is not born of a great battle or a cataclysmic event, but from a moment of profound spiritual imbalance, a time when the pride of the gods threatened to unravel the very fabric of existence. It is a story not of destruction, but of illumination, where divine humility becomes the most potent weapon.

The tale of Sureshwar begins in the celestial realm, after the Devas, the gods, had achieved a monumental victory. For ages, they had waged a ceaseless war against the Asuras, the demons, for control of the universe. The conflict was long and brutal, marked by periods of triumph and devastating loss. But now, after a grueling final battle, the Devas emerged victorious. The great Asura king had been vanquished, and peace and order were restored. The heavenly city of Amravati shimmered with an unparalleled radiance, and the gods, led by the mighty Indra, the king of heaven, reveled in their glorious triumph.

However, with this victory came a fatal flaw: arrogance. The gods began to believe that their triumph was a result of their own strength and power alone. They forgot the cosmic forces that had guided them. They overlooked the divine interventions that had protected them. They ignored the supreme, benevolent power of the Trimurti—Brahma, Vishnu, and Shiva—who maintained the balance of the universe. Brahma had blessed them with boons, Vishnu had provided cunning strategy, and Shiva, the all-pervading consciousness, had ensured their victory by his sheer will. Yet, in their hubris, the gods saw only their own might. Indra was overcome by a blinding sense of pride. He declared in the great assembly of gods, "Did we not, by our own hands, vanquish the foe? Are we not the lords of the universe, the unassailable protectors of *dharma*? The universe now bows before our power alone."

From his abode on Mount Kailash, Lord Shiva, the all-knowing and ever compassionate, observed the gods' descent into arrogance. He knew that this spiritual imbalance was far more dangerous than any demonic threat. A prideful god is a dangerous god, for his actions are no longer guided by righteousness but by ego. To prevent a catastrophe and to restore the cosmic order, Shiva decided to teach the gods a lesson in humility. He chose to manifest not in his fearsome, destructive form, but as a simple, serene being, a humble ascetic whose outward appearance would belie his immense power. This was the genesis of the Sureshwar avatar.

Assuming the form of a radiant, yet unassuming, sage, Shiva placed himself in the gods' path. As the Devas, led by Indra, returned to their celestial city in a grand procession, they came upon this strange ascetic. He stood motionless, his form radiating an inner calm that was as powerful as a mountain. His presence was so immense that it caused the great procession to halt. The gods, filled with their own sense of grandeur, were affronted by this seemingly insignificant being who dared to block their path.

"Who are you, and why do you obstruct our way?" Indra thundered, his voice laced with the arrogance of a victorious king.

The ascetic, Sureshwar, merely smiled, a serene and gentle expression that held the weight of all creation. "I am but a simple wayfarer," he said, his voice calm and melodic. "I am traveling the path of consciousness. It seems we have both arrived at the same place, though our destinations are vastly different."

Indra, unable to comprehend the subtle insult, scoffed. He commanded Agni, the god of fire, to remove the ascetic from their path. Agni, with a flash of fiery arrogance, unleashed his most potent flames, a blaze that could melt mountains and dry up oceans. But as the flames approached Sureshwar, they simply dissipated, as if consumed by a cool, unmoving void. Agni was stunned. His power, the very essence of his being, had been rendered useless. Ashamed, he returned to the procession, his fiery light dimmed.

Next, Indra commanded Vayu, the god of wind, to blow the ascetic away. Vayu, with a gust that could flatten forests and conjure storms, unleashed his full power. But the winds, no matter how forceful, swirled around Sureshwar, unable to even stir the dust at his feet. Vayu, too, returned defeated, his mighty winds a mere whisper.

The other gods, in their turn, attempted to challenge the sage, each failing spectacularly. The god of water found his torrents evaporating; the god of thunder found his bolts dissolving into harmless light. The gods were bewildered. Their most potent powers, the very foundations of their divine authority, were powerless before this simple ascetic. The air around them began to feel heavy with a sense of unease.

Finally, Indra himself, his pride wounded and his patience gone, stepped forward. He raised his most powerful weapon, the **Vajra**, the thunderbolt forged from the bones of a sage, a weapon that had defeated the mightiest of Asuras.

"You have humiliated my gods and dared to defy me, the King of all Devas," Indra roared, his eyes blazing with fury. "Now, you will face the might of my Vajra, a power no one has ever withstood!"

The ascetic, Sureshwar, looked at the fearsome weapon with a gentle smile. He extended his right hand, a gesture of quiet acceptance. As Indra hurled his Vajra with all his celestial might, it sped through the air, crackling with cosmic energy. But as it reached the open palm of the ascetic, it did not detonate. It did not shatter. Instead, it became a tiny, weightless flower, a humble lotus that rested serenely on his palm. The flower, which had once been a weapon of immense destruction, was now a symbol of peace and beauty.

The entire universe held its breath. The gods were struck dumb. Indra, in a single, crushing moment, understood the full extent of his folly. His greatest weapon, the symbol of his power and authority, had been disarmed by a single, simple gesture. His arrogance evaporated, replaced by a deep, shuddering terror. He fell to his knees, trembling.

At that moment, the serene ascetic's form began to change. His skin radiated a transcendental light. A third eye, the eye of cosmic wisdom, opened on his forehead. The divine symbols of a trident, a crescent moon, and a serpent appeared. Before the terrified gods stood Lord Shiva, the Mahadev, in his Sureshwar form. He was not a destroyer now, but a compassionate teacher.

"O Devas," Shiva's voice resonated, a sound that was both thunder and a gentle whisper. "Your victory was great, but it was not yours alone. The power of your weapons, the might of your arms, all are but fragments of a single, cosmic force that pervades all creation. You believed you were the doers, the originators of your own strength. In your pride, you forgot the ultimate source of all power, the one who provides you with the energy to breathe, to fight, and to conquer."

He continued, his words penetrating their very souls. "All the elements—fire, air, water, and earth—are but manifestations of my will. Your Vajra, which you hold as the supreme weapon, is but a fleeting display of my creative energy. I am the very essence that grants you power, and I can withdraw it in a moment. You are not the masters of the universe. You are its guardians, and your duty is to protect it with humility, not with pride. A true protector acknowledges a power greater than their own, for it is from that source that their strength flows."

With this divine revelation, the gods were completely humbled. They prostrated themselves before the Lord, begging for forgiveness. They understood that their greatest weakness was not a lack of power, but a lack of humility. Shiva, in his Sureshwar form, blessed them, restoring their confidence while instilling in them a newfound respect for the cosmic order. The lotus that had once been the Vajra now bloomed, a symbol of the transformation of arrogance into humility.

The Sureshwar avatar of Shiva is a timeless lesson. He is a reminder that even in victory, one must remain humble. He is the quiet presence behind all cosmic phenomena, the guiding force that ensures balance. His story teaches us that true strength is not in the power one wields, but in the wisdom to know its source, and the humility to acknowledge that one is but a fragment of a greater, more profound whole. This story of Sureshwar, therefore, is not a grand epic of battle, but a subtle and beautiful narrative of spiritual awakening, where a god becomes a teacher to the gods, reminding them that the path of consciousness is the true and only destination.

Chapter 19: The Brahmachari Avatar - A Test of Pure Devotion

Among the many awe-inspiring tales of Lord Shiva's avatars, the story of the **Brahmachari** stands as a profound testament to the power of unwavering devotion and the futility of external power without inner purity. This is not a story of cosmic battles or grand acts of creation, but a subtle and deeply personal narrative of spiritual tests. The Brahmachari avatar is a manifestation of Shiva's role as the ultimate ascetic, the master of yogic discipline, who descended to Earth to test the resolve of his most ardent devotee, Goddess Parvati, and in doing so, taught a timeless lesson about the true nature of love and devotion. It is a tale that reminds us that the path to the divine is not paved with grandeur, but with the quiet strength of the heart.

The story begins with the tireless penance of Goddess Parvati. She was the divine consort of Shiva in her previous life as Sati, who had sacrificed herself in a fire, unable to bear the insult to her husband. Now reborn as the daughter of the mountain king Himavan, she was destined to be reunited with Shiva. But Shiva, lost in deep meditation on Mount Kailash, was indifferent to her mortal existence. Undaunted, Parvati decided that she would win his heart through the most difficult of all paths: fierce penance. She forsook all worldly comforts. She ate nothing but dry leaves and endured the bitter cold of the Himalayan winter and the scorching heat of the summer sun. Her singular focus was to purify her soul and prove her worthiness to be Shiva's companion. Her devotion was so intense that it shook the very foundations of the cosmos. All the gods, goddesses, and sages marveled at her unwavering resolve.

While Parvati's penance was a beautiful act of devotion, it was also a test for Shiva himself. A true master does not grant a boon easily; he tests the devotee's sincerity to ensure their devotion is not for a fleeting desire, but for a profound, eternal bond. Lord Shiva, in his infinite wisdom, understood that Parvati's love was pure, but he needed to demonstrate this purity not just to the universe, but also to her. He needed to reveal to her the deeper meaning of their union, which was not about a worldly marriage, but a merging of two supreme cosmic forces. So, he decided to appear before her, not as the majestic and fearsome Mahadev, but in a subtle and unassuming form.

One day, as Parvati sat in deep meditation amidst the snow-capped peaks, she saw a young, radiant ascetic approaching her. He had a gentle smile, a face that radiated wisdom and peace, and his body was lean from years of disciplined living. He was the Brahmachari avatar of Lord Shiva. The Brahmachari was a perfect ascetic, a master of self-control, and he approached Parvati with an air of respectful curiosity. He praised her for her rigorous penance, acknowledging the immense hardship she was enduring. Parvati, a perfect host even in her austere state, welcomed him and inquired about his purpose.

The Brahmachari then asked her a seemingly simple but profoundly significant question: "O noble one, your beauty and piety are unmatched. Your penance is so severe that it is beyond the comprehension of even the gods. Who is it for? For what great boon do you seek to perform such a difficult act?"

Parvati, with a look of pure devotion, answered, "I seek to win the heart of Lord Shiva. I wish to be his wife."

Upon hearing this, the Brahmachari's gentle demeanor changed. He began to speak of Shiva in a manner that was both a critique and a test. He spoke of Shiva not as the supreme deity, but as an eccentric, almost unsettling figure. He described Shiva as an ascetic who lived in cremation grounds, with his body smeared with ashes. He pointed out that Shiva had no home, no wealth, and wore a simple tiger skin. He questioned Parvati's choice, arguing that a woman of her beauty and royal lineage deserved a husband who was a king, a god of great wealth and power, like Indra or Vishnu, not a disheveled ascetic who wandered the forests. He questioned the logic of her love, suggesting that she was perhaps misguided or foolish.

The Brahmachari's words, though harsh, were a test of Parvati's devotion. Would she be swayed by the conventional standards of the world? Would she falter in her love for Shiva because of his unconventional appearance and lifestyle? The Brahmachari's arguments were compelling, rooted in worldly logic and a seemingly rational concern for her well-being. But Parvati's love for

Shiva was not of the world. Her love was for his essence, for his supreme consciousness, for the spiritual truth that he embodied.

Parvati listened patiently. Her heart ached at the insults leveled against her beloved, but her resolve did not waver. With quiet dignity, she looked at the Brahmachari and said, "O Brahmachari, I have listened to your words with respect. But you speak of Lord Shiva as a stranger. You do not know him. You speak of his appearance, his possessions, and his home, but these are merely external illusions. The true Shiva is the ultimate reality. He is the one who holds the universe in his being. He is the source of all existence. His ashes are the remnants of all creation, and his simple living is a testament to his detachment from all worldly desires. His home is the universe itself."

She continued, "I do not seek a worldly king. I seek the king of yogis, the one who is beyond all worldly attachments. My love for him is not because of his wealth or power, but for the truth that he represents. You, a scholar and a sage, should know that what is seen with the eyes is not always the truth. The true essence of a being is found in their soul. I do not care for his appearance or his possessions; I care for the supreme consciousness that he is. No amount of worldly comfort could ever compare to the spiritual bliss of being united with him."

As Parvati spoke, her voice was filled with a passion that came from the depths of her soul. Her words were a divine revelation, a testament to a love that was pure, unconditional, and transcended all worldly concerns. The

Brahmachari was deeply moved. He saw in her a devotion so profound that it was beyond any test. He saw that her love was not for a person, but for a principle. Her love for Shiva was her own self-realization, her own journey towards the supreme truth.

At that moment, the Brahmachari's disguise fell away. His true form, that of the magnificent Lord Shiva, was revealed. His third eye shone with divine light, and a serene smile of supreme satisfaction was on his lips. He gently took Parvati's hand and spoke to her with a voice that was both a caress and a command. "O Parvati, your penance has been successful. You have passed the ultimate test. Your devotion is as pure as the light of the sun and as firm as the Himalayas themselves. You have understood the true essence of my being, and in doing so, you have become one with me. You have shown the entire universe that true love is not about external appearance or worldly possessions, but about the profound connection of the soul."

Lord Shiva's Brahmachari avatar is a powerful and timeless lesson. It teaches us that our devotion to the divine, or to any person or principle, should not be based on external factors. True devotion is an internal state, a conviction that is so strong it can withstand any critique, any doubt, and any test. The Brahmachari's apparent insults were not meant to hurt Parvati, but to strengthen her resolve and to demonstrate her unwavering love to the world. He showed her that the path to spiritual union is not about performing grand acts, but about having a heart so pure and a faith so strong that it becomes an unshakeable mountain. The Brahmachari's story, therefore, is not about the defeat of a demon, but about the triumph of a pure heart over the illusions of the world. It is a testament to the idea that the greatest power of all is the power of a devotion that knows no bounds.

Chapter 20: The Unbound Saviour : Avadhut Avatar

In the vast pantheon of Hindu deities, where divine beings manifest to uphold dharma, the **Avadhut** avatar of Lord Shiva stands apart. Unlike the warrior avatars who descend to fight demons and restore balance with force, the Avadhut saves the universe through a profound and silent act of renunciation. This is a story not of a physical battle, but of a cosmic awakening, where the saviour's ultimate power lies in his complete detachment from the world he protects. He is the unbound one, a divine paradox whose very existence is a beacon of ultimate truth.

The term **Avadhut** itself means "one who has shaken off" or "one who is cast off." It refers to a state of absolute spiritual freedom, a being who has transcended all worldly attachments, social norms, and egoic identity. While other avatars embody specific qualities like valour, righteousness, or love, the Avadhut embodies the raw, untamed essence of Shiva—the pure consciousness that remains untouched by creation, preservation, and dissolution. He is a living representation of non-duality, a state where there is no separation between the self and the divine. This avatar does not appear in a specific epoch to fulfill a singular prophecy; rather, he is a timeless principle, manifesting whenever the universe's crisis is one of spiritual ignorance and suffocating attachment.

The cosmic crisis that summons the Avadhut is not a war waged by a demon, but a far more insidious threat: the collective delusion of Maya. As the cycles of existence turn, humanity often loses its way, becoming enslaved by desire, ego, and the illusion of a separate self. This spiritual malaise chokes the very lifeforce of the universe, leading to moral decay, conflict, and suffering. It is a time when external saviours are insufficient, for the true enemy lies within the hearts of beings. To combat this, Lord Shiva, the Mahadeva, takes the form of the Avadhut to remind the cosmos of its true, boundless nature. He is the ultimate physician for the soul, prescribing the bitter but liberating medicine of truth.

The Avadhut's appearance is a powerful symbol of his purpose. He is often depicted naked, smeared with ashes, with long, matted hair. He carries no possessions, lives without shelter, and wanders freely, indifferent to praise or scorn. This outward appearance is a stark and deliberate defiance of all societal conventions. The ashes symbolize the impermanence of the physical world, reminding all that everything, from the mightiest king to the lowliest beggar, will one day turn to dust. His nakedness represents a complete lack of shame, fear, or attachment to the physical body. He is a living challenge to the ego, an embodiment of the fearless, pure spirit. By living outside the established order, the Avadhut provides a counter-narrative to a world that has become lost in its own rules and illusions. His very presence forces beings to question their definitions of success, happiness, and salvation.

The most profound aspect of the Avadhut's saving grace is his teaching by example. He does not deliver long sermons or write scriptures. Instead, his teachings are conveyed through his actions, which are often spontaneous, unpredictable, and seemingly eccentric to the conventional mind. He might appear as a madman, laughing without reason, crying without sorrow, or eating from a rubbish heap. These actions are not random; they are masterful lessons in detachment. He demonstrates that joy and sorrow, clean and unclean, rich and poor are all constructs of the mind. By treating everything with equal indifference, he shows the path to true liberation from duality. The essence of his message is that salvation is not an achievement to be gained, but a state of being to be realized—the innate, blissful nature of the self.

One of the most famous incarnations of the Avadhut principle is **Lord Dattatreya**, often revered as a manifestation of the Hindu Trimurti—Brahma, Vishnu, and Shiva—in a single body. Dattatreya's story perfectly illustrates the Avadhut's role as a universal guru. He wandered the world, taking twenty-four gurus from nature itself, from a bee to a child to a spider. This narrative highlights the Avadhut's limitless wisdom and his ability to find a lesson in every aspect of existence, showing that enlightenment is not confined to sacred texts or a single path. His simple, profound life was a continuous lesson on the futility of material pursuit and the boundless wisdom available to those who observe the world without judgment. Through Dattatreya, the Avadhut teaches that the entire universe is a potential teacher, and true salvation lies in constant, mindful observation and introspection.

The Avadhut's role as a saviour becomes critically important during times of spiritual darkness. While a warrior avatar might vanquish a tyrant, the root cause of the tyranny—the collective ego and ignorance—often remains. The Avadhut addresses this root cause directly. His presence is a subtle but potent force that purifies the cosmic consciousness. He is the ultimate force of cleansing, not through destruction, but through profound spiritual insight. When a person encounters the Avadhut, their life is irrevocably changed. His gaze can dissolve illusions, his silent presence can still the mind, and his seemingly random acts can shatter a lifetime of conditioning. He is a living mirror, reflecting back to beings their true nature, encouraging them to cast off the chains of their own making.

In essence, the Avadhut avatar is Shiva's most powerful and paradoxical expression of universal salvation. He is a saviour who saves by refusing to be a saviour. He offers no promises, no rituals, and no easy answers. His only offering is the unvarnished truth of existence. He does not fight external enemies; instead, he helps each individual to confront and conquer their internal ones—the desires, attachments, and ignorance that bind them to suffering. The Avadhut is the embodiment of the final liberation, the ultimate state of freedom. He is a beacon for all who seek to transcend the cycles of birth and death, a living testament to the fact that the greatest power in the universe is not the ability to control, but the courage to let go. His eternal presence reminds the universe that salvation is not a destination, but a state of being—a state of pure, unbound consciousness, just like the Mahadeva himself.

Chapter 21: The Rudra Avatar – Hanuman, The Universal Saviour

In the vast, interconnected tapestry of Hindu mythology, where divine energies manifest in countless forms, few connections are as profound or as revered as that between Lord Shiva and Hanuman. Known as the Rudravatar, a fiery emanation of the Mahadeva himself, Hanuman is more than just a loyal devotee of Lord Rama; he is the very embodiment of Shiva's power, wisdom, and selfless devotion. His story is not merely that of a valiant monkey-god, but a profound narrative of a cosmic force born to restore dharma and protect the universe from the forces of chaos.

The genesis of this divine union traces back to a time of profound cosmic crisis. The universe groaned under the weight of adharma, personified by the tyrannical rule of Ravana, the ten-headed rakshasa king. Ravana, a great scholar and a devotee of Shiva, had accumulated immense power through penance, but his ego had warped his divine gifts into tools of cruelty and oppression. The gods, tormented and powerless, approached Lord Vishnu, who promised to descend to Earth as Lord Rama to vanquish the darkness. Yet, the task was so immense that it required not just the power of Vishnu, but the formidable, destructive, and regenerative energy of Shiva. Thus, by divine will, Shiva, the eternal yogi, agreed to manifest a portion of his essence to aid Vishnu in his earthly mission.

Shiva chose the form of an eleven-faced Rudra to destroy the forces of evil. The eleventh Rudra is considered the most powerful and the most benevolent of the eleven Rudras, embodying the ultimate protective and transformative power of Shiva. He was to be born to Anjana, a celestial nymph cursed to live as a vanara, and Kesari, the vanara king. It is said that when Vayu, the wind-god, was carrying a sacred offering intended for the birth of Lord Rama, a small portion was snatched by a kite and deposited in Anjana's palm. Anjana consumed this divine food, and from it, impregnated with the essence of Shiva and the grace of the gods, she gave birth to a child of unparalleled strength and divine purpose. This child, named Hanuman, was destined to be the living embodiment of Shiva's Rudra energy—a cosmic force of righteous fury and boundless compassion.

From his very birth, Hanuman demonstrated his divine nature. Mistaking the sun for a ripe fruit, he leaped towards it, a testament to his boundless energy and audacious spirit. This act, while seemingly childlike, was a foreshadowing of his universal significance. He was not just an individual; he was a manifestation of cosmic principle. His body, strong as a thunderbolt, and his spirit, as free and untamable as the wind, were gifts from his divine lineage. He was indestructible, capable of changing his form and size, and imbued with incredible speed and strength. These powers, however, were not for self-aggrandizement, but were the tools of a saviour. They were the arsenal of Shiva, wielded for the protection of dharma and the restoration of universal harmony.

The purpose of Hanuman's avatar became clear when he encountered Lord Rama in the forest of Kishkindha. From their very first meeting, an instant, unshakeable bond of love and loyalty was formed. Hanuman, in a posture of complete surrender, recognized in Rama the supreme Lord, the very form of Vishnu. It was in this moment that Hanuman's true purpose as a universal saviour began to unfold. His role was not to lead armies or to rule kingdoms, but to serve as the bridge between the divine and the mortal, between power and humility.

Hanuman's most pivotal act of cosmic salvation came during the search for Sita. Ravana's abduction of Sita was not merely a personal injustice; it was a cosmic imbalance, a symptom of the darkness that had consumed the world. The search for her was a desperate quest that had broken the spirit of the vanara army. It was here that Hanuman's role as the eleventh Rudra became evident. He possessed the power and will to accomplish what no other could. With a single, breathtaking leap across the vast ocean to Lanka, Hanuman demonstrated his universal power. He traversed the boundaries of worlds, defied the laws of nature, and faced countless supernatural beings, not with ego, but with an unwavering focus on his divine mission. In this act, he was not just a messenger; he was the embodiment of hope, the force that pierced through the veil of impossibility to bring light to a dark and hopeless situation.

Upon his return, Hanuman brought more than just news of Sita; he brought renewed purpose to Lord Rama and the entire vanara army. His actions in Lanka—setting the city ablaze and single-handedly destroying a portion of Ravana's forces—were a display of Shiva's fiery destructive energy, but a destruction that was necessary for the sake of creation. This was the Rudra at work: a force of righteous destruction clearing the path for a new era of peace and light.

Hanuman's role as a saviour extended beyond the battlefield. During the great war, when Rama's brother Lakshmana was mortally wounded, it was Hanuman who undertook the most desperate and crucial mission. The only cure was the Sanjeevani herb, found on a remote Himalayan mountain. Facing a seemingly insurmountable task against time and distance, Hanuman once again invoked his divine essence. He flew with incredible speed, not just to the mountain, but when he couldn't identify the herb, he lifted the entire mountain itself. This act was not just a feat of physical strength, but an act of universal compassion. He saved not just one life, but the entire divine mission, for without Lakshmana, Rama's resolve would have been broken. In this moment, Hanuman was a saviour of saviours, ensuring that the ultimate divine purpose of the Rama avatar would be fulfilled.

Hanuman's existence is a profound teaching on the nature of divinity. His power is a direct reflection of Shiva's might, yet it is his unwavering humility and selfless service to Rama that makes him truly divine. He is the cosmic protector who never seeks glory. His identity is intrinsically tied to his purpose—to serve and to protect. This is the essence of his role as the eleventh Rudra, an avatar of Shiva whose power is not for destruction, but for the preservation of dharma.

Even after the war, Hanuman did not seek the heavenly abode or a position of power. He chose to remain on Earth, a living embodiment of faith and devotion, a protector of those who seek the path of truth. His presence is felt wherever the name of Rama is chanted, a constant reminder that divine power is best wielded in the service of love and devotion. In every act of his life, from his birth to his eternal vigil, Hanuman has proven to be the ultimate saviour—a force of Shiva's will, born to rescue not just a kingdom, but the very essence of universal righteousness. His is a story of power without ego, devotion without end, and a salvation that continues to resonate through the ages.

Chapter 22: The Nataraja Avatar: The Cosmic Dance of Salvation

In the vast and intricate iconography of Hinduism, few images are as iconic or as philosophically profound as that of **Nataraja**, or **Nateshwar**, the Lord of the Dance. He is not merely an avatar who appears to fight a singular demon or solve a temporary crisis; he is the embodiment of Shiva's eternal dance, a cosmic performance that is the very engine of the universe. This dance is a powerful, ongoing act of salvation, preserving the cosmos from stasis and ensuring the perpetual cycle of creation, preservation, and dissolution. To understand Nataraja is to understand that the universe is not a static place, but a vibrant, ever-changing drama, and that salvation is an unending process of movement and transformation.

The genesis of the Nataraja avatar is rooted in a fundamental cosmic crisis: the threat of ultimate ignorance and illusion. In one of the most famous myths, Shiva descends to the forest of Daruvana to subdue a group of arrogant sages. These sages, proud of their rituals and knowledge, had lost sight of the ultimate reality. To challenge their ego, Shiva appears as a beautiful mendicant, accompanied by Vishnu as his beautiful consort. Enraged by Shiva's disregard for their asceticism, the sages send a series of magical attacks against him. They conjure a fierce tiger, which Shiva effortlessly subdues and skins, wrapping its hide around his body. Next, they unleash a venomous serpent, which Shiva tames and wears as an ornament. Finally, the sages summon **Apasmara**, the demon of ignorance and forgetfulness, a dwarf-like being who embodies spiritual blindness.

This is the pivotal moment of the dance. As Apasmara charges, Shiva simply places his foot upon the dwarf's back, pinning him to the ground. This single act is the central message of the Nataraja avatar: he does not destroy ignorance; he subdues and controls it. **Apasmara is not killed because ignorance cannot be eliminated from the universe.** It is a necessary part of the cosmic play, a challenge that allows for the pursuit of wisdom. By pinning the demon, Shiva shows that while ignorance is a constant threat, it can be overcome and transcended. This act is the ultimate form of salvation for the universe—not the physical destruction of evil, but the eternal subjugation of spiritual darkness, allowing all beings to seek light.

The cosmic dance itself is an intricate performance of five divine actions, known as the **Panchakritya**. These five actions are the very forces that sustain and regenerate the cosmos:

1. **Srishti (Creation):** Represented by the drum held in his upper right hand, Shiva's dance begins with the rhythmic beat that brings all of existence into being. The sound of the drum is the primordial vibration, the first moment of creation that saves the universe from an unending state of non-existence.

2. **Sthiti (Preservation):** The lower right hand is held in the **abhaya mudra**, the gesture of "fear not." This hand grants protection and reassurance to his devotees, promising that the cosmic order will be maintained. It is the force that preserves the universe he has created, a saving act that provides stability and continuity.
3. **Samhara (Destruction):** In his upper left hand, Shiva holds a flame. This flame is the fire of dissolution, the force that consumes the universe at the end of each cycle. It is a saving act, for destruction is not an end but a clearing, a necessary prelude to a new beginning. Without this creative destruction, the universe would become stagnant and corrupted, unable to renew itself.
4. **Tirobhava (Concealment/Illusion):** The left arm, which crosses his chest in the **Gajahasta** ("elephant trunk") pose, symbolizes the cosmic illusion that hides the ultimate truth. This is the veil of Maya that makes the spiritual journey difficult but meaningful. It is a saving act because it provides the challenge and the purpose for spiritual evolution, guiding souls from ignorance to wisdom.
5. **Anugraha (Grace/Liberation):** His raised left foot, which is lifted in the dance, represents the promise of liberation. It is the foot that dances above the demon of ignorance, offering a path

for all beings to escape the cycle of birth and death. The grace of Nataraja is the ultimate act of salvation, offering the final release from all suffering and illusion.

Through this perpetual dance, Shiva is the constant, active saviour of the universe. He is a dynamic deity, not a static one. The dance is not a one-time event; it is a continuous process that is happening at every moment, in every atom of the cosmos. The rotation of planets, the changing of seasons, the cycle of life and death—all are part of Nataraja's eternal performance. His presence ensures that the cosmos will never fall into a state of decay.

The saving grace of the Nataraja avatar is not a single, dramatic rescue. It is a perpetual, rhythmic force that sustains, protects, and ultimately liberates. He saves the universe by being its very life force, the cosmic pulse that ensures that from destruction, new life will always emerge, and from ignorance, wisdom will always be sought. He teaches us that salvation is not something to be earned in a distant heaven but is a dynamic process of transformation that is constantly available to those who seek it within the cosmic dance of life.

Chapter 23: The Bhikshuvarya Avatar: The Path of Divine Humility

In the grand pantheon of Hindu mythology, Lord Shiva is revered in countless forms, from the fierce destroyer **Rudra** to the serene meditator **Dakshinamurti**. Yet, among his myriad avatars, one of the most paradoxical and philosophically profound is **Bhikshuvarya**, the Divine Mendicant. This form is not associated with epic battles against demons or dramatic rescues from cosmic floods. Instead, the Bhikshuvarya avatar's act of salvation is subtle, internal, and aimed at a more insidious cosmic threat: the pervasive darkness of arrogance and spiritual ignorance. His story is a powerful reminder that the universe can be saved not by a sword, but by a begging bowl, and that true power lies not in acquisition but in total surrender.

The cosmic crisis that necessitated Shiva's descent as a beggar was not a physical one but a spiritual one. In a time when the universe was seemingly in balance, the **Devas** (celestial beings) and even the great sages had begun to lose their way. They had become intoxicated by their own power, their knowledge, and their celestial status. The sages, proud of their rigorous penance and mystical achievements, began to believe that their powers were their own doing, forgetting that all divine grace flows from the ultimate reality. This pervasive sense of ego, of "I," threatened to unravel the very fabric of the cosmos, replacing humility with hubris and spiritual pursuit with self-aggrandizement. The universe was heading towards a spiritual collapse, where beings, convinced of their own self-sufficiency, would forget their divine origin and the true path to liberation.

To correct this cosmic imbalance, Lord Shiva manifested as **Bhikshuvarya**, the Divine Beggar. He appeared as a simple, unadorned mendicant, covered in sacred ash, his hair matted and his eyes radiating a serene, detached wisdom. He carried nothing but a begging bowl, and his every step was a lesson in non-attachment. This was a deliberate act of divine theater. The supreme Lord, who is the source of all wealth and all existence, was now going door-to-door, begging for a few morsels of food. The very sight of the Lord of the Universe in such a humble form was a profound challenge to the ego of the gods and sages.

Bhikshuvarya's journey was a sacred pilgrimage through the illusion of ownership. He went to the very heavens and the hermitages of the proud sages, asking for alms. His act was not out of need, but out of divine compassion. By humbling himself, he was offering them a path to salvation. The act of giving to a beggar, especially to the one who is the Lord of All, forces the giver to surrender their sense of ownership. It breaks the illusion that one's wealth, knowledge, or power is a personal possession. In that moment of giving, the giver is confronted with the stark reality of their own impermanence and the ultimate source of all things.

The ultimate act of salvation performed by Bhikshuvarya was the direct subduing of the ego. This is a far more fundamental and lasting act of salvation than simply destroying a physical demon. The ego is the root cause of all suffering and the greatest obstacle to spiritual enlightenment. By manifesting as a beggar, Shiva was not fighting an external enemy; he was performing an internal surgery on the collective cosmic consciousness. He taught beings that salvation is found not in accumulating, but in renouncing; not in power, but in humility; not in seeking, but in giving. This act saved the universe from the cycle of self-destruction brought on by pride and greed.

The symbolism of the Bhikshuvarya avatar is rich with meaning. The begging bowl, or **Bhikshapatra**, is a cosmic vessel that represents the universe itself. The food that is placed in it represents the sustenance and energy of all creation. By holding the bowl, Shiva shows that he is the ultimate recipient and consumer of all things. He accepts the offerings of the universe, but he also consumes and dissolves them, ensuring that nothing becomes permanent or corrupts the cosmic balance. The sacred ash, which he is often depicted with, symbolizes the ultimate state of all things—the formless reality that remains after all material existence has been consumed. This serves as a constant reminder of the impermanence of the material world and the eternal nature of the divine.

In some traditions, Bhikshuvarya is also depicted alongside Vishnu in the form of the beautiful **Mohini**. This companionship adds another layer of profound meaning to the story. Mohini represents the captivating and seductive power of Maya (cosmic illusion), which makes the world of forms appear real and desirable. By having Maya accompany him on his rounds,

Bhikshuvarya shows that the path of renunciation is not about escaping the world, but about navigating its illusions with divine detachment. The two together represent a holistic view of the divine—that creation and illusion (Maya) are as much a part of the divine play as renunciation and detachment.

In conclusion, the Bhikshuvarya avatar stands as a powerful testament to Shiva's multifaceted role as a cosmic saviour. He did not defeat a physical foe, but instead, he corrected a spiritual crisis that threatened to consume all of existence. By embodying the path of total humility and renunciation, he saved the universe from its own self-destructive tendencies. His story is a timeless lesson that true salvation is not an external event, but an internal transformation. He reminds us that the greatest strength is found in our ability to let go, that the most divine act is giving, and that the path to liberation is walked with nothing but a humble spirit and an empty begging bowl.

Chapter 24: The Kshemaka: The Avatar of Universal Welfare

In the vast and multifaceted tradition of Shaivism, Lord Shiva is revered in countless forms, each revealing a different aspect of his divine nature. Among these, the avatar known as **Kshemaka** is particularly significant, though his story is less celebrated in popular mythology. His name, derived from the Sanskrit word *kshema*, means "welfare," "security," and "prosperity." This avatar is not a warrior who descends to fight a single demon, nor is he a teacher who imparts spiritual wisdom. Instead, Kshemaka's act of salvation is perhaps the most fundamental: he appears to bring peace and stability to a universe plagued by discord, fear, and a profound lack of harmony.

The cosmic crisis that necessitated Shiva's descent as Kshemaka was not a battle of gods versus demons, but an internal decay of the cosmos itself. In this period, a deep-seated imbalance had set in. The divine order, or **Dharma**, was not being actively threatened by a powerful tyrant, but was slowly unraveling due to mutual suspicion, moral decay, and a pervasive sense of insecurity. Beings, from celestial deities to humble mortals, lived in a state of perpetual anxiety. Minor disputes erupted into major conflicts, alliances dissolved, and the very fabric of trust that held the universe together began to fray. The celestial spheres were filled with unease, the elements of nature were restless, and the hearts of all living beings were clouded by fear. This was a crisis of existence itself, a state where the universe was not being actively destroyed but was silently suffering from a loss of its foundational security.

To address this profound cosmic suffering, Lord Shiva did not manifest in a form of power or wrath. Instead, he appeared as **Kshemaka**, a gentle, serene figure radiating an aura of profound peace. He was depicted with a calming gaze, his hands often holding symbols of well-being, such as a staff of protection or a pot containing the nectar of amity. His presence was not intimidating; it was comforting. As Kshemaka, he did not command or force order; he inspired it. His arrival was like the first morning light after a long, restless night, bringing with it a sense of hope and tranquility that was desperately needed.

The act of salvation performed by Kshemaka was subtle yet transformative. Instead of engaging in combat, he traveled throughout the cosmos, his mere presence instilling a deep sense of security and trust. His method was to restore the inherent harmony of the universe by acting as a living embodiment of peace. He would appear in the midst of warring factions, not as a judge, but as a silent observer. His serenity would gradually disarm the combatants, and they would find their anger and animosity fading away. His wisdom was shared not through long discourses, but through simple gestures and a compassionate gaze. He taught beings that true strength lies not in domination, but in cooperation; and that lasting prosperity is not about winning a conflict, but about creating an environment where everyone can thrive.

Kshemaka's salvation was a lesson in the power of empathy and the importance of **collective welfare**. He showed that the well-being of the individual is inextricably linked to the well-being of all. His journey was a testament to the idea that a peaceful existence is a divine right, and that it is the responsibility of every being to contribute to the harmony of the whole. He intervened in the forces of nature, calming storms and restoring the balance of the elements. He guided the celestial beings back to their sacred duties, reminding them of the interconnectedness of their roles. In essence, he was the great restorer, the divine anchor that pulled the universe back from the brink of chaotic self-destruction.

The symbolism of the Kshemaka avatar is rich with meaning, highlighting the profound nature of his role. His serene posture represents the tranquility that comes from inner balance. The staff he holds is not a weapon, but a symbol of his unwavering support for justice and righteousness. His compassionate gaze reminds all beings that they are under the constant and benevolent watch of the divine. The very name **Kshemaka** serves as a mantra for protection and prosperity. This avatar teaches us that Shiva's divine dance of cosmic order is not just one of destruction and creation, but also one of sustained peace and security.

In conclusion, the Kshemaka avatar offers a powerful and unique perspective on the nature of divine salvation. He did not defeat a physical enemy, but instead healed the deep-seated spiritual and emotional wounds of the cosmos. By embodying the principles of welfare and security, he reminded all beings that the path to liberation is paved not with conquest, but with compassion. He proved that the universe can be saved not by a display of cosmic force, but by a simple, loving presence that brings peace to every heart. His story is a timeless lesson that the greatest form of divine intervention is the one that restores our trust in one another and in the ultimate benevolence of the universe itself.

Chapter 25: Durvasa: The Avatar of Divine Fury

Among the most unconventional and profound of avatars is the avatar of **Durvasa**, the irascible sage. While most avatars are celebrated for their acts of compassion, heroic battles, or profound teachings, Durvasa is known for his fiery temper and his seemingly disproportionate curses. Yet, to understand Durvasa is to understand a deeper form of divine salvation, one that operates not through gentle guidance but through a shocking and powerful corrective force. His fury is not a sign of imperfection but a surgical tool used to cleanse the universe of the most dangerous cosmic ailment: the ego. The universe is not saved by a sword or a boon, but by the swift and purifying fire of his rage.

The cosmic crisis that necessitated Shiva's descent as Durvasa was not a physical threat from a powerful demon but a spiritual plague that had begun to rot the foundations of the cosmos. Over time, the celestial beings and great sages had become complacent and arrogant. The gods, basking in their immortality and power, had forgotten their place in the divine hierarchy. The sages, proud of their austere penances and mystical powers, began to believe that their strength was their own, rather than a gift of divine grace. This collective hubris threatened to unravel the very fabric of **Dharma** (cosmic law), leading to a state of moral decay where respect for the divine and for each other was lost. The universe was on a path to spiritual stagnation, a state where beings would become so lost in their own pride that they would forget their ultimate purpose.

To counter this subtle but pervasive threat, Lord Shiva manifested as **Durvasa**, a being whose name literally means "one who is difficult to live with." He was a walking storm, an embodiment of the cosmic principle that balance must be maintained, even if it requires a drastic and uncomfortable correction. His appearance was often disheveled, covered in sacred ash, with matted hair and a gaze that could either bless or burn. His role was to be a mirror, reflecting the arrogance of others back to them, and his curses were not acts of petty revenge but precise instruments of cosmic justice designed to humble and purify.

One of the most famous examples of Durvasa's role as a saviour through anger is his encounter with **Indra**, the king of the gods. As the story goes, Durvasa was gifted a garland by the celestial nymph **Prabhavati**. He was pleased with the offering and, in turn, presented the divine garland to Indra. However, Indra, in his arrogance, was sitting on his elephant, **Airavata**, and casually placed the garland on the elephant's trunk. The fragrant garland was so divine that it attracted a swarm of bees, and Airavata, annoyed by the bees, threw the garland to the ground and stomped on it.

Durvasa was enraged. He saw this act not as a simple mistake, but as a profound insult to the sanctity of the divine offering and a symptom of Indra's deep-seated pride. He immediately cursed Indra and all the gods to lose their strength, their fortune (**Lakshmi**), and their immortality. The gods were stripped of their powers and became vulnerable, paving the way for the demons to defeat them and take control of the universe. This curse seemed destructive, but it was, in fact, a saving grace. It was the shock that the gods needed to wake up from their slumber of self-importance. It forced them to seek the help of **Vishnu** and, in doing so, to engage in the epic event of the **Samudra Manthana** (the churning of the cosmic ocean). From this great churning, not only did the gods regain their lost powers and immortality, but the universe was also gifted with countless treasures, including the nectar of immortality and the goddess Lakshmi herself. Durvasa's curse was the catalyst that saved the universe from the slow, spiritual decay that their pride had initiated.

Another compelling story that illustrates Durvasa's role is his encounter with **King Ambarisha**. Ambarisha was a great devotee of Vishnu, renowned for his piety and adherence to religious fasts. One day, after completing a strict **ekadasi** fast, he was about to break his fast when Durvasa arrived. Ambarisha respectfully welcomed the sage and offered him a meal. Durvasa agreed to eat but first went to the river to perform his ablutions, leaving Ambarisha waiting. As the time to break the fast was about to expire, Ambarisha was faced with a dilemma: if he broke the fast before the guest ate, he would be disrespecting the sage, but if he didn't, he would break his vow of fasting. After consulting with his priests, he decided to take a small sip of water to technically break the fast without consuming a meal.

Durvasa, upon his return, immediately sensed what had happened. He flew into a divine rage, feeling that his hospitality had been insulted and that the king's act was a display of subtle arrogance. He created a fierce demoness from his matted hair to attack the king. However, Vishnu's divine discus, the **Sudarshana Chakra**, appeared and protected Ambarisha. The Chakra pursued Durvasa relentlessly, forcing him to flee in terror. He sought refuge with Brahma and Shiva, but neither could help him. Finally, he went to Vishnu himself, who told him that the only way to be saved was to seek forgiveness from the very person he had wronged, King Ambarisha. Durvasa, humbled and terrified, did so, and the king immediately forgave him.

In this story, Durvasa's anger again acts as a cosmic correction. His wrath exposes the ultimate power of divine devotion and the principle of **surrender** to the higher power of Vishnu. It teaches that even the most powerful ascetic, filled with the fire of penance, is ultimately subject to the greater cosmic law of devotion. Durvasa's humiliation was a lesson for everyone: pride and spiritual power are nothing before true faith. By humbling himself, Durvasa was not only saved from the Sudarshana Chakra but was also spiritually corrected, fulfilling his own role as a divine agent.

In conclusion, the **Durvasa** avatar is a complex and often misunderstood aspect of Shiva's nature. He is not a whimsical or petty figure but a profound teacher and a powerful saviour. His curses and his anger are not destructive acts but are tools of purification, designed to break the spiritual diseases of arrogance and pride that threaten to unravel the cosmic order. He saves the universe not by fighting an external enemy, but by confronting the internal demons within gods, sages, and mortals alike. The stories of Durvasa are a constant reminder that the path to salvation is not always comfortable and that the divine can intervene in the most shocking and unexpected ways to bring us back to the path of **Dharma**. His is a brutal but necessary grace, and through his fury, he ensures the spiritual health and long-term stability of the cosmos.

Chapter 26: Khandoba: The Warrior of Justice

In the vast and ever-expanding narrative of Hindu mythology, Lord Shiva manifests in a multitude of forms, each designed to address a specific cosmic need. From the ferocious destroyer **Rudra** to the benevolent householder **Gangadhara**, his avatars are as diverse as the challenges they face. Among these, the avatar known as **Khandoba** is a powerful testament to Shiva's capacity for direct and tangible salvation. Primarily revered in the Deccan plateau of India, Khandoba's story is deeply rooted in local folklore, blending the supreme deity with the spirit of a protective folk hero. His act of salvation is not a philosophical teaching or a cosmic dance, but a clear-cut, decisive battle to restore justice and protect the innocent. He is the guardian who saves the universe by physically subduing the forces of chaos and establishing a kingdom of peace and security.

The cosmic crisis that necessitated Shiva's descent as Khandoba was a terrestrial one, but its implications threatened the balance of the entire universe. Two formidable demon brothers, **Malla** and **Mani**, had risen to power. Through intense and rigorous penance, they had acquired extraordinary boons from the gods, which made them virtually invincible. Armed with their newfound power, they unleashed a reign of terror upon the three worlds. Malla, the elder, was a symbol of pure tyranny and ego. He demanded that all beings worship him and not the gods. Mani, his younger brother, was a more subtle but equally dangerous force, representing spiritual ignorance and moral decay. Their combined arrogance and brutality shattered the harmony of the world, tormenting sages, disrupting rituals, and bringing a deep sense of fear to all living beings.

As their torment grew unbearable, the gods and sages, powerless against their boons, turned to Lord Shiva for help. He alone possessed the power to overcome the demons' invincibility. In response to their pleas, Shiva manifested in a form that was both divine and earthly: the avatar of **Khandoba**. His name itself is a testament to his purpose, derived from the Sanskrit word *khadga*, meaning "sword," and *bhu*, meaning "earth" or "being." He appeared as a majestic warrior, mounted on a magnificent white horse, his face radiating a fierce but compassionate resolve. He was accompanied by his consort, **Mhalsa**, and his faithful dog, both of whom played a crucial role in his mission. This was a striking departure from Shiva's more common forms. He was not a meditating ascetic or a cosmic dancer but a king and a warrior, fully prepared to engage in a physical battle to restore order.

The battle that ensued between Khandoba and the demon brothers was a defining moment of this avatar's purpose. He engaged Malla and Mani in a fierce and prolonged conflict. Malla, in his arrogance, was certain of his victory, but Khandoba's sword, the **Khanda**, was no ordinary weapon. It was a tool of divine justice, imbued with the power to sever the bonds of ego and ignorance that made the demons so formidable. The battle was a dramatic clash of order against chaos, justice against tyranny. Khandoba's every move was a lesson in righteous anger and unwavering purpose. He did not engage in philosophical debates; he delivered a swift and direct correction to the forces that were disrupting the universe.

In the final moments of the battle, Khandoba defeated Malla, beheading him with his divine sword. Mani, seeing his brother fall, was humbled and terrified. He surrendered to Khandoba and asked for forgiveness. In a moment that reveals the compassionate heart behind the warrior's fury, Khandoba spared Mani. However, before he was granted salvation, Mani had one final request: that he be allowed to be reborn as a protector of Khandoba's devotees. Khandoba granted this wish, and Mani was transformed, forever serving the very force he once fought against. This act of grace shows that while Khandoba's primary role is to punish evil, his ultimate goal is to redeem and re-establish harmony, even for his foes.

Khandoba's act of salvation is unique because it is so tangible and relatable. He saved the universe not by abstract means, but by protecting the physical well-being of its inhabitants. His avatar teaches a powerful lesson: sometimes, the greatest act of divinity is to take up a sword, not out of hatred, but out of a profound and unwavering commitment to justice. He is the guardian who ensures that the world is a safe place for spiritual and material life to flourish. The victory over Malla and Mani was not just the end of a demonic reign but the beginning of an era of security and faith. His temples, particularly the one in **Jejuri**, became centers of pilgrimage and community, places where devotees could seek his protection and receive his blessings for their families and their well-being.

In conclusion, the **Khandoba** avatar stands as a powerful and beloved manifestation of Lord Shiva. He is the embodiment of righteous action, demonstrating that the divine can and will intervene to protect its creation from even the most destructive of forces. His story is a timeless reminder that while spiritual battles are fought in the heart, the security of the physical world is also a sacred responsibility. He is the warrior of justice, the protector of the innocent, and the one who saves the universe by ensuring that evil is not just contained, but swiftly defeated. He is Shiva in a form that all can understand, a loving protector who wields a sword with unwavering purpose and boundless grace.

Chapter 27: Kirateshwar: The Test of the Divine Archer

In the vast tapestry of Hindu mythology, where the divine and the mortal realms often intersect, Lord Shiva's incarnations are not merely tales of power but profound lessons in devotion, humility, and the true nature of divinity. Among these, the story of the Kirateshwar Avatar holds a special place, not for its grandeur in a cosmic war, but for its subtle yet supreme act of saving the universe from the folly of a righteous warrior. This is the tale of how the all-powerful Mahadev, the Lord of ascetics and destruction, chose the form of a simple tribal hunter to test the greatest archer on Earth and in doing so, averted a catastrophe.

The story unfolds after the monumental dice game in the epic Mahabharata, a game that sealed the fate of the Pandava princes. Stripped of their kingdom and honor, the five brothers—Yudhishthira, Bhima, Arjuna, Nakula, and Sahadeva—were exiled to the forest for twelve years. While his elder brothers resigned themselves to their fate, Arjuna, the peerless archer and the most valiant of the Pandavas, found his spirit restless. The disgrace of his family and the unquenchable thirst for justice gnawed at his soul. He knew that to win back their kingdom and restore dharma, they would need a power far greater than what they possessed. With the counsel of the great sage Vyasa, Arjuna resolved to seek divine weapons from the gods. His ultimate goal was to obtain the most potent of all, the **Pashupatastra**, a weapon so destructive that its mere presence could annihilate all creation.

To obtain such a weapon, one needed to prove not only immense valor but also supreme self-control and devotion. Guided by Vyasa, Arjuna embarked on a rigorous journey to a hermitage in the Himalayas, a place where the gods often resided. He left behind all worldly comforts, his princely robes, and his royal life. Clad in simple ascetic garb, he began a period of intense penance, a spiritual practice designed to cleanse the body and mind. Days turned into weeks, and weeks into months. Arjuna stood on one leg, enduring the biting cold winds, the relentless rain, and the scorching sun. He subsisted on air and his unwavering determination.

His penance was so profound that it disturbed the cosmic balance. The heat generated by his austerities caused the earth to tremble and the skies to glow. Even the mighty gods, seated in their celestial abodes, felt the tremors and grew concerned. Was this mortal man attempting to usurp their power? Lord Indra, Arjuna's celestial father, was particularly worried. He sent Apsaras, divine celestial nymphs, to distract Arjuna with their unparalleled beauty and charm, but Arjuna remained steadfast in his meditation, his focus unyielding. Impressed, Indra blessed him and urged him to seek the divine favor of Lord Shiva directly.

Meanwhile, an incredibly powerful and arrogant demon named Mooka, the son of the demon king Hiranyaksha, decided to take advantage of Arjuna's deep meditation.

Mooka, disguised as a wild boar with tusks as sharp as daggers, charged towards Arjuna, intending to disrupt his penance and kill him. The boar was no ordinary beast; it was a demonic entity of great power.

At this very moment, Lord Shiva, observing everything from his divine abode on Mount Kailash, decided to intervene. He was pleased with Arjuna's unflinching devotion and valor but also saw the arrogance lurking beneath the surface, an ego that could become a grave danger if he were to wield a weapon as powerful as the Pashupatastra. A weapon of that magnitude could not be given to someone who was not yet a master of his own ego. To test Arjuna and teach him a final, critical lesson, Lord Shiva transformed himself. He shed his divine form of the meditating yogi and took on the appearance of a Kirata—a wild, muscular tribal hunter.

With him was his consort, Goddess Parvati, who had also taken the form of a Kirati huntress. Shiva, in his Kirata form, was dark-skinned, with matted hair adorned with peacock feathers and a bow and arrow in hand. He was surrounded by his *ganas* (attendants), who appeared as a group of hunters.

As the wild boar charged at the meditating Arjuna, both the hunter and the prince shot their arrows simultaneously. The two arrows, one from the hunter and one from the ascetic, struck the boar at the same time. The demon fell, its demonic form dissipating, leaving its physical form on the forest floor.

An immediate and heated dispute arose. Both Arjuna and the Kirata hunter claimed to have slain the beast.

“It was my arrow that took him down!” Arjuna declared, his voice filled with pride and a hint of impatience.

“Nonsense!” the hunter scoffed. “Did you not see my arrow, the one that struck him first? The boar belongs to me, for I am a hunter, and this is my prey.”

Their argument escalated into a full-blown war of words, followed by a fierce physical battle. Arjuna, confident in his unparalleled skill, unleashed a barrage of arrows, each one aimed with the precision that had earned him the title of the world's greatest archer. To his astonishment, the hunter dodged every single one with impossible agility. Arjuna's divine arrows, which had felled countless enemies, were rendered useless against this mysterious tribal man.

Realizing that this was no ordinary mortal, Arjuna's pride began to crumble. He resorted to using his celestial weapons, one after another, but the hunter countered each weapon effortlessly. The battle was a cosmic dance of power and skill, but it was clear to everyone watching from the heavens that the hunter was toying with Arjuna. Frustrated and exhausted, Arjuna's mind was humbled. He finally laid down his bow and decided to fight the hunter with his bare hands. He lunged at him, but the Kirata, with a playful smile, easily evaded him.

With his weapons failing and his body worn out, Arjuna's arrogance finally gave way to respect. He had been defeated, not by a god, but by a simple hunter. In that moment of complete humility, he realized his mistake. He offered a prayer to Lord Shiva, the very deity he had been seeking, asking for forgiveness and strength.

As Arjuna knelt in devotion, the Kirata hunter's form began to shimmer and transform. The peacock feathers and rugged hunting attire disappeared, replaced by the serene form of Lord Shiva. His matted locks held the celestial river Ganga, a crescent moon rested upon his head, and a third eye shone on his forehead. With a smile that radiated the peace of the cosmos, Shiva stood before his astonished devotee.

“Arjuna,” Shiva's voice boomed with the resonance of a thousand thunderstorms, yet it was as gentle as a flowing stream. “I came to test you. You have performed the greatest penance and shown unmatched valor. But you still had a thread of pride in your heart. A warrior who wields the Pashupatastra must not have even a trace of arrogance. Today, you have defeated your greatest enemy—your ego.”

Arjuna fell at Shiva's feet, his heart overflowing with shame and reverence. He now understood the true nature of his test. It was not about winning a physical battle but about conquering his inner self. Satisfied with Arjuna's transformation, Lord Shiva, the great preserver of balance, granted him the ultimate weapon. He not only gave him the **Pashupatastra** but also taught him the sacred chants and rituals to invoke it.

The Kirateshwar avatar is a profound narrative of divine intervention as a saviour. Shiva did not save the universe through a grand-scale war or by destroying a monstrous demon. Instead, he saved it by preventing a potential future catastrophe. By humbling the greatest warrior of his time and granting him the wisdom to wield divine power responsibly, Lord Shiva ensured that the most potent weapon would be used only when absolutely necessary, under the guidance of righteousness.

This act was a pre-emptive strike against the future misuse of a cosmic weapon, a testament to Shiva's role not just as a destroyer of evil, but as a protector who acts with wisdom and foresight, ensuring the delicate balance of creation remains undisturbed.

Chapter 28: Yaksheswar Avatar: Lesson for the Gods

The universe was at peace. The great churning of the **Samudra Manthan** was complete, and the divine and demonic forces had departed from the cosmic shores. Lord Shiva, having consumed the **Halahala** poison and contained it in his throat, had returned to his meditation on Mount Kailash, his sacrifice the unseen foundation of the new cosmic order.

However, the Devas, the gods of the heavens, had learned a new lesson, and it was not one of humility. The *Amrita* had made them immortal, and with their newfound invincibility, a quiet arrogance began to take root in their hearts. They boasted of their strength, their cunning, and their role in the successful churning, entirely forgetting the help they had received from both Lord Vishnu and, more importantly, the silent sacrifice of Lord Shiva. Their pride swelled, becoming a new kind of poison, unseen but just as corrosive as the *Halahala* that had threatened to destroy all creation.

Lord Shiva, from his deep state of meditation, perceived this spiritual ailment. He knew that this hubris was a far greater danger to cosmic balance than any demon or venom. Without a grounding in humility, the immortal Devas would only grow more reckless and powerful, eventually leading to a disaster far worse than the one they had just averted.

To correct this imbalance, Shiva chose a new form. He did not appear as the fearsome Destroyer or the serene Ascetic, but as **Yaksheswar**, the Lord of the Yakshas. The Yakshas were ancient spirits of the earth, often guardians of hidden treasures and untamed forests. In this form, Shiva took on a gentle, youthful appearance, radiant with a quiet, patient strength that resembled a sturdy mountain rather than a raging fire.

He descended to the heavens and appeared before the Devas, who were in the midst of a grand feast, celebrating their victory. They were surprised to see a stranger among them, a being of immense, yet understated, power. They offered him a seat and asked him who he was.

Yaksheswar simply smiled, his gaze holding the wisdom of a thousand ages. He manifested a single, delicate blade of grass and placed it on the ground. "I have heard of your great power," he said in a soft, melodic voice. "If you are truly as mighty as you say, then break this blade of grass."

The Devas laughed, a sound that echoed with their collective pride. **Indra**, the king of the gods, stepped forward. He called upon his most powerful weapon, the **Vajra**, a thunderbolt capable of splitting mountains. With a mighty roar, he hurled the Vajra at the blade of grass. There was a brilliant flash of light and a deafening sound, but when the dust settled, the tiny green blade stood completely untouched.

Humiliated, Indra retreated. Next came **Agni**, the god of fire, who attempted to burn the grass with his scorching flames, but the fire merely flickered out, unable to even singe the blade. **Vayu**, the god of wind, unleashed a mighty gale that could flatten entire forests, but the blade of grass did not even tremble. All the gods, one by one, attempted to destroy the insignificant blade, but all of their power proved useless.

Finally, they bowed their heads, their arrogance shattered. They realized that their power was not their own, but was merely a borrowed grace from a higher, supreme being. They begged the mysterious Yaksheswar to reveal his true form. With a knowing smile, Yaksheswar vanished, and in his place appeared Lord Shiva, his matted hair and trident unmistakable. The gods fell to their knees in reverence, their hearts humbled and filled with newfound devotion.

The story of Yaksheswar is a timeless reminder that true power is not found in victory or in physical might, but in the quiet strength of **humility** and the wisdom to recognize a higher, guiding force.

Chapter 29: The Vrishbha Avatar: A Tale of Pride and Divine Intervention

The Vrishbha avatar, or bull incarnation, of Lord Shiva is a significant but less-known tale in Hindu mythology, particularly detailed in the **Shiva Purana**. It highlights a conflict between Shiva and Vishnu and underscores Shiva's role as a restorer of cosmic order.

The story begins in the aftermath of the **Samudra Manthan**, the great churning of the cosmic ocean. During this event, gods and demons worked together to retrieve the elixir of immortality, **Amrita**. To prevent the demons from obtaining the Amrita, Lord Vishnu took on the enchanting form of **Mohini**, a beautiful celestial maiden. Mohini captivated the demons, and in their mesmerized state, Vishnu tricked them and distributed the Amrita to the gods.

While in the guise of Mohini, Lord Vishnu descended to the netherworld, **Patala Loka**, to retrieve some of the enchanting beauties who had been captured by the demons. Here, ensnared by the magical illusion he had created, Vishnu became captivated by his own feminine form. In this state of delusion, he fathered a few powerful and arrogant sons with the apsaras. These sons, born of Vishnu's divine essence but also a result of his enchantment, grew up to be mischievous and unruly. They began causing chaos throughout the three worlds, challenging the authority of the gods and disrupting the balance of the universe.

The gods, tormented by the arrogance and destructive actions of Vishnu's sons, went to **Lord Brahma** to seek a solution. Brahma, in turn, led them to **Mount Kailash** to plead with Lord Shiva. Upon hearing of the plight of the worlds, Shiva, the great ascetic and destroyer of evil, decided to intervene. He recognized that this was not a matter for a conventional battle but required a form that could subdue the pride of Vishnu's sons and restore cosmic harmony.

Taking on a unique and formidable form, Lord Shiva transformed into a majestic bull, the **Vrishbha Avatar**. This bull was no ordinary creature; it was colossal, with sharp, destructive horns, a thunderous bellow, and the strength of a hundred mountains. In this form, Shiva descended to the netherworld, roaring and shaking the very foundations of Patala.

Upon seeing the majestic bull, Vishnu's sons, proud of their lineage and strength, rushed to confront him. They were armed with celestial weapons and filled with rage. However, the Vrishbha avatar proved to be more than a match for them. With powerful kicks of his hooves and sharp thrusts of his horns, the divine bull tore through Vishnu's sons. Their bodies were shattered and their lives were extinguished instantly.

When Lord Vishnu learned of the destruction of his progeny, he was filled with rage and emerged to confront the bull himself. A fierce battle ensued between the two supreme deities. Vishnu, the preserver, shot divine arrows and powerful missiles at the Vrishbha avatar. Shiva, in his bull form, met each attack with equal force, kicking the missiles and using his horns to deflect the weapons. The earth trembled, and the heavens watched in awe as the two most powerful gods clashed.

Finally, in a moment of clarity, Vishnu realized the true identity of his opponent. He saw that the mighty bull was none other than Lord Shiva, the very essence of destruction and renewal. Recognizing his own arrogance and the chaos his sons had created, Vishnu surrendered. He praised Shiva for restoring order and acknowledged that it was only through Shiva's intervention that the universe could be saved from the turmoil caused by his progeny.

Shiva, having completed his task, returned to his divine abode on Mount Kailash. The universe was restored to its peaceful state, and the gods rejoiced. The Vrishbha avatar is a powerful reminder that even the most powerful deities are not immune to delusion and that Shiva, as the ultimate ascetic and restorer of cosmic balance, will intervene when pride and chaos threaten the existence of the three worlds.

Chapter 30: Not The End But The Begining

The journey through Shiva's many forms and legends has led us to a profound, and until now, comforting conclusion: that his divine nature is a perfect paradox. We have accepted the rhythm of his cosmic dance—the benevolent saviour who drinks the world's poison, balanced by the fierce destroyer who clears the path for rebirth. It is a cycle that promises balance, no matter the chaos.

In this section, we discussed the avatars of Mahadeva and their significance. Now, I leave it to the readers to decide: is Shiva the saviour of the universe or its destroyer?

The remaining aspects will be discussed in the next part of the book.

About The Author

Advocate Satyabrata Mohanty

Advocate Satyabrata Mohanty is an advocate by profession, but by passion, he is a devoted writer and a lifelong seeker of spiritual wisdom. He holds a deep reverence for Indian mythology, philosophy, and the timeless stories of the divine. Fascinated by the enigmatic figure of Lord Shiva—the saviour, the destroyer, the yogi, the cosmic dancer—he has spent years exploring ancient texts and delving into the symbolic depths of Shaivism.

Through this book, Advocate Satyabrata Mohanty invites readers on a journey beyond mythology, into the essence of Shiva as both a cosmic force and a deeply personal guide to transformation, inner stillness, and awakening.

When not writing, he can be found advocating in courts, studying law or mythological texts, teaching, traveling to spiritual sites, or simply sitting in silence under the stars, contemplating the mysteries of existence.

www.ingramcontent.com/pod-product-compliance
Lightning Source LLC
Chambersburg PA
CBHW062141160726
48282CB00027B/890
* 9 7 8 9 3 5 6 7 9 8 7 6 2 *